W9-BNQ-867

Extraordinary Jobs in

HEALTH AND SCIENCE

Also in the Extraordinary Jobs series:

Extraordinary Jobs for Adventurers
Extraordinary Jobs in Agriculture and Nature
Extraordinary Jobs with Animals
Extraordinary Jobs for Creative People
Extraordinary Jobs in Entertainment
Extraordinary Jobs in the Food Industry
Extraordinary Jobs in Government
Extraordinary Jobs in Leisure
Extraordinary Jobs in Media
Extraordinary Jobs in the Service Sector
Extraordinary Jobs in Sports

Extraordinary Jobs in

HEALTH AND SCIENCE

ALECIA T. DEVANTIER & CAROL A. TURKINGTON

Ferguson

An imprint of Infobase Publishing

Extraordinary Jobs in Health and Science

Ferguson
An imprint of Infobase Publishing
132 West 31st Street
New York NY 10001

Library of Congress Cataloging-in-Publication Data

Devantier, Alecia T.
  Extraordinary jobs in health and science / Alecia T. Devantier and Carol A. Turkington.
    p. cm.
  Includes index.
  ISBN 0-8160-5858-X (hc : alk. paper)
  1. Allied health personnel—Vocational guidance—Juvenile literature. 2. Science—Vocational guidance—Juvenile literature. I. Turkington, Carol. II. Title.
  R697.A4D48 2006
610.69—dc22   2006008418

Ferguson books are available at special discounts when purchased in bulk quantities for businesses, associations, institutions, or sales promotions. Please call our Special Sales Department in New York at (212) 967-8800 or (800) 322-8755.

You can find Ferguson on the World Wide Web at http://www.fergpubco.com

Text design by Mary Susan Ryan-Flynn
Cover design by Salvatore Luongo

Printed in the United States of America

VB KT 10 9 8 7 6 5 4 3 2 1

This book is printed on acid-free paper.

CONTENTS

Acknowledgments. vii
Are You Cut Out for a Career
   in Health and Science?. ix
How to Use This Book xii

Acupuncturist 1
Aromatherapist 4
Art Therapist. 7
Astronaut. 10
Astronomer 13
Crime Scene Examiner. 16
Criminologist 19
Cryonics Researcher 22
Cryptographer 25
Document Examiner. 28
Dolphin Researcher 31
Entomologist. 35
Fingerprint Analyst 38
Fire Scientist 41
Flight Nurse 44
Forensic Sculptor 47
Gemologist 51
Geriatric Care Manager 54
Herpetologist 57

Historical Interpreter 61
Hospital Chaplain. 64
Hypnotherapist. 67
Laughter Therapist. 71
Massage Therapist 74
Medical Aesthetician. 77
Medical Illustrator 79
Mental Health Advocate 83
Midwife. 86
Museum Display Designer 89
Palliative Care Professional 92
Parasitologist 95
Perfusionist 98
Phlebotomist. 101
Physical Therapist 104
Scientific Inventor 108
Set Medic 112
Venom Researcher. 116
Virologist 120

Appendix A. Associations,
   Organizations, and Web Sites. . .123
Appendix B. Online Career
   Resources 143
Read More About It. 151
Index 157

ACKNOWLEDGMENTS

This book wouldn't have been possible without the help of countless others who referred us to scientists and health experts, and who came up with information about a wide variety of odd and unusual jobs. We deeply appreciate the time and generosity of all those special people in the health and science field who took the time to talk to us about their unusual jobs.

Thanks also to all the people who helped with interviews and information and the production of this book, including Susan Shelly McGovern, editors James Chambers and Sarah Fogarty, Vanessa Nittoli, agents Ed Claflin of Ed Claflin Literary Associates and Gene Brissie of James Peter Associates, and to Michael and Kara, and Mike, Sara, and Ryan.

ARE YOU CUT OUT FOR A CAREER IN HEALTH AND SCIENCE?

If you love math and science or you have a desire to help people in some way, perhaps you've thought about becoming a doctor, nurse, or research scientist—certainly these are all terrific jobs in the fields of health and science. But there are far more jobs in these fields beyond the obvious that many kids never even consider. And that's why we've written this book.

Do you spend every waking moment thinking and dreaming about space? Have you always been fascinated with the way dolphins communicate, ever since that first episode of *Flipper*? Do you love the idea of helping babies come into the world, but you're drawn more to the alternative end of medicine? Are you a whiz at art and science and wish there was a way to combine the two? Ask yourself: *What am I passionate about*?

If you follow your heart, you're almost guaranteed to find a career in science and health that you'll love. In fact, almost every individual we interviewed for this book repeated the same litany—*I love my job. It's different. It's unusual. It's unique.*

Many unusual jobs in health and science are every bit as difficult and require just as much training as the more traditional careers. What these more unusual jobs offer, however, is something much harder to measure—a job that lets your spirit soar and allows you to do what you love to do.

Of course, loving what you do is only part of having a successful career. You've also got to be good at what you want to do. Most of these jobs are so specialized that if you're going to go after one of them, you need to be very good at it and have some specific training. Whether you're thinking of becoming a parasitologist or a flight nurse, you need to have the talent and the training to do that job better than most other people.

Chances are, if you're like most of us, you've inherited a bevy of *shoulds*. These *shoulds* inside your head can be a major stumbling block in finding and enjoying a career in health or science. Maybe other people won't be so happy with your career choice. You may hear complaints from your family and friends who just can't understand why you don't want a "regular job." They want you to be a doctor, but you're thinking more about acupuncture. If you confide your career dreams to some of these people, they may try to discourage you. Can you handle their continuous skepticism or downright disappointment? Other people often have their own *shoulds* for you, too.

Or maybe you're having a hard time imagining a different path for yourself because of the obstacles you see. Maybe you're saying to yourself: "There's just no way I can follow my dream and make a living . . . I don't have the right background . . . I'm the wrong sex . . . I'm the wrong color." Think again! Sally Ride didn't accept anyone's idea that a woman can't be an astronaut. You, too, can be successful if you choose not to accept others' assessments. If you get bogged down in the belief that you can't follow your dream because of what *is*, you take away your power to discover what *could be*. You lose the power to create a different future for yourself.

Almost everyone we've talked to in the process of writing this book has ended up with an unusual job in health or science by a circuitous route. A few people have always known exactly what they wanted to do, and did it. But for the rest of us, it can take years to work up the courage to actually do what we knew all along we would have loved to do.

You don't have to start big. You don't have to wake up one day and decide to study infectious diseases in the Amazon rainforest. Start with a chemistry class. Check out a couple of books. Try an internship or unconventional summer job. Travel. Volunteer. "The best thing you can do as a young investigator is to look at different perspectives and use as many different scientific disciplines as possible, and bring it into a field where you think you'd like to do research," says venom researcher Jon-Paul Bingham. "I still use my pathology, my toxicology, my biochemistry, organic chemistry, all these fields I've learned. This way, you become a unique scientist. Some people segment the different fields, but if you bring them all together, it will help you make connections."

Ultimately, you've got to work hard. Many scientists and health experts say that one of the most important things in their development was to find a good mentor— somebody who can see your potential and invites you into the lab to work together.

"No scientist is an island," Dr. Bingham says. "We must be able to jump from one island to another, make bridges, be able to discuss science together. This way, someone may see the same problem from a different perspective and that will open the door of opportunity."

Too many kids don't realize how many different, exciting jobs there are in the health and science fields. In fact, everything you see around you—your toothpaste, eye drops, the shoes you wear, the car you drive—all were developed by experts in the fields of physics, mathematics, chemistry, biochemistry, medicine, pharmacology.

There is so much in the world that we haven't yet developed, and so much potential to make our lives better. Just consider what amazing strides this country has made in the last 100 years! In 1900, there was no radio or TV, no computers or iPods, no videotapes or videogames, no CDs or DVDs. There were no air conditioners, no neon lights, no airplanes or helicopters, no lasers, no windshield wipers, no tractors. There were no radar or sonar, no cellophane, no talking motion pictures, no crossword puzzles, no bras or zippers, no stainless steel, no nylon or ballpoint pens, no toasters or Band-aids, no robots or lie detectors, no traffic signals, microwave ovens, or mobile phones. There were no frozen foods, bubble gum, cornflakes, cake mix, McDonald's, diet soft drinks, instant coffee, or Pez.

TV wasn't invented until 1925; yo-yos in 1929; Scotch tape, the jet engine, and the analog computer in 1930. Parking meters came along in 1931, and drive-in movies in 1933. Jeeps weren't invented until 1940, scuba diving equipment in 1943.

In the early 20th century, there were no vaccinations against measles, mumps, German measles, polio, pneumonia, hepatitis, rabies, flu, or meningitis. Many people died of everyday bacterial infections because antibiotics weren't invented until 1940, and many more died of TB until a cure was found in 1944. Until that year, you could die of kidney problems because there was no kidney dialysis. Scientists didn't know smoking caused lung cancer until 1950, or that fluoride could prevent cavities until 1951. Until 1965 you were stuck with glasses, because there were no contact lenses. Many people with heart disease died before the invention of the artificial heart in 1969.

How far we've come in just 100 years! Your great-grandparents most likely lived without electricity in homes lit by oil lamps, cooked with woodstoves, butchered their own meat and grew their own food, used horses for transportation. If they traveled abroad, they did so only by ship—and then only if they were wealthy. They probably sewed their own clothes, made their own soap, and had babies in their own homes.

Just 100 years later, we're sending probes to Jupiter, performing microsurgery, and attaching severed limbs—even whole new faces—to grievously injured patients.

"We have made so much progress in the last 40 years that it gives me the shivers to think what the next generation of new scientists are going to come up with," says Dr. Bingham. "What I discover today may turn into someone's magnificent discovery for tomorrow. That's why we have

to protect the environment, and make sure humankind doesn't destroy things where the potential is still undiscovered."

Try not to think of learning and working as two totally separate things. When somebody hands you a diploma, you don't stop learning. School can be the best place to build up your fact-based knowledge; the rest of your life provides you with experience-based knowledge. You need both the facts and experience to forge an unusual career in health and science. Take charge of your journey instead of relying on someone else's career path. Take advantage of the things you learn as you plan your next experience.

You may encounter setbacks along the way. How do you handle adversity? How do you feel when you fail? If you've always wanted to be an astronomer, how are you going to feel if you have trouble getting into graduate school or no one seems to want to hire you? If you can pick yourself up and keep going, you've probably got the temperament to survive the rocky road to an unusual health or science career.

Learn to look at the world through curious eyes, whether that takes you to the depths of the microscopic world or the limitless reaches of outer space. By exploring your options, you'll learn that work and play become the same thing. Push past your doubts and fears—and let your journey begin!

Carol A. Turkington
Alecia T. Devantier

HOW TO USE THIS BOOK

Students face a lot of pressure to decide what they want to be when they grow up. If you're not interested in a traditional job but you're still fascinated by the health and science fields, where can you go to find out about these exciting careers?

For example, you may have wondered where you can go to find out how to become an acupuncturist or an aromatherapist, exploring alternative medicine. What does it take to become a medical artist, illustrating complex procedures in medical textbooks? Where do you learn how to conduct research with dolphins? Is it really possible to make a living as a gemologist? What sorts of things would you be doing as a virologist? What's the job outlook for medical skin care specialists?

Look no further. This book will take you inside the world of a number of different jobs in health and science, answering questions you might have, letting you know what to expect if you pursue that career, introducing you to someone making a living that way, and providing resources if you want to do further research.

THE JOB PROFILES

All job profiles in this book have been broken down into the following fact-filled sections: At a Glance, Overview, and Interview. Each offers a distinct perspective on the job and taken together give you a full view of the job in question.

At a Glance

Each entry starts out with an At a Glance box, offering a snapshot of important basic information to give you a quick glimpse of that particular job, including salary, education/experience, personal attributes, requirements, and outlook.

✅ *Salary range.* What can you expect to make? Salary ranges for the jobs in this book are as accurate as possible; many are based on data from the U.S. Bureau of Labor Statistics' *Occupational Outlook Handbook*. Information also comes from individuals, actual job ads, employers, and experts in the field. It's important to remember that salaries for any particular job vary greatly depending on experience, geographic location, and level of education. For example, a midwife in a small town will earn far less than his or her colleague in a big-city ob-gyn practice.

✅ *Education/Experience.* What kind of education and experience does the job require? This section will give you information about such requirements.

✅ *Personal attributes.* Do you have what it takes to do this job? How do you think of yourself? How would someone else describe you? This section will give you an idea of some of the personality traits that might be useful in this career. These attributes were collected from articles written about the job, as well as recommendations from employers and people actually working in the field.

✅ *Requirements.* Are you qualified? Some jobs, particularly those with the government, have strict age or education requirements.

✅ *Outlook.* What are your chances of finding a job? This section is based in part on the *Occupational Outlook Handbook*, as well as interviews with employers and experts doing the jobs. This information is typically a "best guess" based on the information that is available right now, including changes in the economy, situations in the country and around the world, job trends and retirement levels, and many other factors that can influence changes in the availability of these and other jobs. For example, 10 years ago the job outlook for a medical skin care specialist would not have been nearly as rosy as it is today, with the explosion of revolutionary skin care treatments, such as acid peels, new types of lasers, and all sorts of anti-aging products and procedures.

Overview

This section will give you an idea of what to expect from the job on a day-to-day basis. For most of these jobs, there is no such thing as an average day. Each new day or new assignment is a whole new adventure with a unique set of challenges and rewards.

The overview also discusses how to get into the profession. It takes a more detailed look at the required training or education, giving an in-depth look at what to expect during that training or educational period. If there are no training or education requirements for the job, this section will provide some suggestions for getting the experience you'll need to be successful.

No job is perfect. **Pitfalls** takes a look at some of the obvious and not-so-obvious drawbacks. Don't let the pitfalls discour-

age you from pursuing the career; these are just things to be aware of while making your decision.

For many people, loving your job so much that you look forward to going to work every day is enough of a perk. **Perks** looks at some of the other benefits of the job you may not have considered.

So what can you do *now* to start working toward the career of your dreams? **Get a Jump on the Job** will give you some ideas and suggestions for things that you can do, even before graduation, to start preparing for this job. Opportunities include training programs, internships, and organizations to join, as well as practical skills to learn and courses to take.

Interview

In addition to taking a general look at the job, each entry features a discussion with someone who is lucky enough to do this job for a living. The experts give you an inside look at the job and offer advice to those interested in pursuing a career in the same field.

APPENDIXES

Appendix A (Associations, Organizations, and Web Sites) lists places to look for additional information about each specific job, including professional associations, societies, unions, government organizations, Web sites, and periodicals. Associations and other groups are a great source of information about jobs in the health or science field, and there's an association for just about every job you can imagine.

Many groups and associations have a student membership level, which you can join by paying a small fee. There also are lots of advantages to joining an association, including the chance to make important contacts, receive helpful newsletters, and attend workshops or conferences. Some associations also offer scholarships that will make it easier to further your education. Other sources listed in this section include information about accredited training programs, forums, official government links, and more.

Appendix B (Online Career Resources) lists some of the best general Web sites about unusual jobs in health and science. Use these as a springboard to your own Internet research. All of this information was current when this book was written, but Web site addresses do change. If you can't find what you're looking for at a given address, do a simple Web search—the page may have been moved to a different location.

READ MORE ABOUT IT

In this back-of-the-book listing, we've gathered some helpful books that can give you more detailed information about each job we discuss in this book. Find these at the library or bookstore if you want to learn even more about careers in health and science.

ACUPUNCTURIST

OVERVIEW

Acupuncture is the practice of inserting needles into a patient's body to treat pain or illness. Using techniques developed in traditional Chinese medicine, the acupuncturist not only eases pain but also can prevent illness and promote health. The acupuncturist inserts very fine needles into specific, targeted spots of the patient's body, which stimulates certain areas and responses. Acupuncturists may also use massage and mild electric stimulation.

Acupuncture works very well for headaches, neck pain, nausea caused by chemotherapy and other factors, carpal tunnel syndrome, sinus problems, arthritis, asthma, depression, and many other conditions. It's particularly advantageous for patients who for various reasons can't tolerate surgery or medications.

Acupuncturists may work in private practice or with a group of other practitioners. Some acupuncturists team up with massage therapists, chiropractors, herbalists, or other specialists in order to be able to provide a more comprehensive level of care to patients.

Acupuncture requires significant skill and training and therefore requires various certifications. Acupuncturists must be able to assess problems in patients and thoroughly understand where to place the needles in order to treat particular problems. This requires sound knowledge of the functions of organs, muscles, and the circulatory system.

To diagnose a patient's condition, an acupuncturist may check pulse rate and

temperature, observe the person's overall appearance, and examine various parts of the body, such as the tongue and fingernails. While Western medicine often tends to use a one-size-fits-all approach to treating sickness, traditional Asian medicine looks at the particular circumstances of each patient. For instance, an 18-year-old athlete and an 80-year-old widow both suffering from back pain most likely require much different methods of treatment. While the 18-year-old probably suffered a back injury while working or participating in sports, the recently widowed 80-year-old may be suffering from depression, which contributes to the pain. An acupuncturist would spend a significant amount of time talking to both patients to determine

Dr. Heidi Klingbeil, acupuncturist

Heidi Klingbeil was licensed as a medical doctor before she went back to school and received training as an acupuncturist. The reason she looked to acupuncture to supplement her medical skills, she says, was because she wanted to be able to quickly and effectively help her patients suffering from pain.

"I treat a lot of pain in my work as a doctor, and we often don't have a good answer for pain," Klingbeil says. "It's not a good answer to tell someone in pain that he'll just have to wait. When you get a haircut, or have your hair dyed, you leave with a souvenir of the visit. But when a person who's in pain comes to the doctor, he doesn't want to leave with a souvenir of that pain. He wants to get rid of it. And acupuncture can do that."

Klingbeil oversees an integrated medical center on the campus of the University of Colorado Health Sciences Center and teaches courses in the university's medical program, in addition to her work in acupuncture. When she's working as an acupuncturist at the center, which she describes as a sort of outpatient clinic, most of the day is spent with patients.

"You see a train of patients with varying problems," Klingbeil says. She'll take time with each patient to discuss the location, nature, and duration of the pain, complete a medical history, and examine symptoms. She also tries to find out what's going on in her patients' lives. "Sometimes," she notes, "the pain will be related to other events in their lives. Acupuncture has a definite, proven chemical effect," Klingbeil says. "It's a natural chemical effect, but it causes results."

Once she has established what's going on, she gets out her needles. "It's just a matter of putting needles at points where the pain is," Klingbeil says. "If somebody points to a spot and says it hurts, you're going to put a needle there for sure. And you also treat the points in the hands and the feet that relate to that pain."

Klingbeil's skills as an acupuncturist have made her popular with her neighbors, who look to her when they're in pain. She's also been known to treat her son's basketball teammates to relieve pain from shin splints. "If any of my neighbors have a fender bender, they're over to my house, asking me to put in a few needles," she says.

Klingbeil recommends that anyone interested in being an acupuncturist attend an accredited school. But she cautions that although acupuncture is becoming more accepted, acupuncturists still don't earn the same respect that medical doctors enjoy. However, if you really want to help patients and be able to effectively relieve pain, acupuncture is a great field, she says. "You won't have the esteem that an M.D. does, but that's okay," she says. "Acupuncture is a lot of fun, and boy, does it work well!"

where the pain is coming from and the best way to treat it.

Acupuncture has been proven to work well in alleviating certain types of pain and conditions, such as nausea. Western society has become more accepting of acupuncture and other complementary and alternative forms of medicine as research has proven their worth and they have become more regulated.

As with most medical practitioners, an acupuncturist must be willing to tend to the administrative aspects of the job, such as maintaining patient files and charts. Some acupuncturists, especially those just starting out in their own practices, even handle scheduling of appointments and other administrative duties.

Pitfalls

As with any type of medical job, you are responsible for the well-being of your patients, and mistakes can have very serious consequences. This causes significant pressure and stress for some medical practitioners. Being an acupuncturist requires a great deal of education, which will be expensive. Beginning acupuncturists may not earn as much as they'd like. If you plan on a private practice, you'll need to work hard to become known and establish a good reputation.

Perks

Acupuncturists often see immediate and dramatic results in their patients' conditions, which can be extremely rewarding. You may be able to set your own hours, allowing you a degree of flexibility. With growing interest in and acceptance of the practice of acupuncture, acupuncturists are likely to be in demand in coming years.

Get a Jump on the Job

Read everything you can find about the history and practice of acupuncture. Contact an acupuncturist in your area and ask if you might stop by sometime to ask some questions and find out more about the profession. Most adults are happy to share information about their work with young people.

AROMATHERAPIST

OVERVIEW

If you love plants and flowers and enjoy working with people, you might be interested in a career as an aromatherapist—a specialist in complementary medicine who uses essential oils extracted from plants to improve physical and emotional well-being and help prevent disease.

Aromatherapy is not intended to replace traditional medical care, but can be used to allow nature to help heal the body and mind. Aromatherapy was first practiced by ancient Egyptians and Native Americans.

This natural, noninvasive treatment system uses essential oils to affect a person's entire body, not just treat the symptoms, and to boost the body's natural ability to heal itself.

Essential oils are highly concentrated aromatic extracts distilled from a variety of aromatic plants including roots, grasses, leaves, flowers, needles, twigs, fruit peels, and wood. These oils may be used in many different forms: They can be rubbed into the skin during therapeutic massage, added to a warm bath for relaxation and rejuvenation, or placed in an electronic glass or pottery diffuser or a clay candle to perfume the air and stimulate the senses. Diluted essential oils sprayed onto a compress can be applied to the body to boost healing. The oils can be used in a water spray as an essential oil spritzer, or the aromas can be applied via compress, salves, mouthwash, creams, and gels.

As a type of holistic medicine, aromatherapy can both prevent and treat a wide variety of conditions, such as depression,

ing sunburn), wounds, scars, motion sickness, colds and flu, sore throat, asthma, and bronchitis. Aromatherapy is also used to help heal fungal infections, reduce skin inflammation, and enhance wound healing.

Many countries today embrace aromatherapy, especially where natural therapies are more widely accepted. In France, aromatherapy is part of the course of study for getting a medical degree, and in Japan, many employers and stores use energetic scents to keep workers and shoppers happy.

grief, anxiety, insomnia, lack of concentration, irritability, memory, moodiness, panic attacks, tension, and worry. It can also be used for bruises, sprains, burns (includ-

Kelly Holland-Azzaro, aromatherapist, R.A.

Even as a teenager, Kelly Holland-Azzaro was interested in holistic medicine and oils and scents. "I drove my parents crazy," she says, "trying to avoid products that had been tested on animals." She became interested in aromatherapy, massage, and yoga in high school and received some aromatherapy and massage treatments from a chiropractor. It seemed only natural for her to seek a career in the natural healing arts. She began to read about aromatherapy, became more interested, and eventually studied with world-renowned aromatherapists for more than 20 years. Today she has her own line of aromatherapy products, Ashi Aromatics.

Holland-Azzaro is a massage therapist and aromatherapist who works together with her husband, an acupuncture physician, in their healing center, Ashi Therapy, in Banner Elk, North Carolina. There she concocts her own products (and offers more than 100 for sale) as part of her business. She's also the vice president of the National Association for Holistic Aromatherapy.

Introducing the scents of essential oils into the atmosphere can have almost an immediate effect on a client. When you inhale a scent, Holland-Azzaro says, the properties of an essential oil help to produce an effect on your mood.

"I love my work," she says. "I love the smells, and what I really love is that even one smell can turn somebody on to the benefits of aromatherapy. I love working with them and seeing them have a positive outcome: Sharing with others and helping others to see how something so simple can have such a positive effect on their life."

She cautions clients to make sure their aromatherapist is well trained. "A lot of people don't have the training and they don't know anything about the chemical combinations or whether the client has allergies and how oils can affect that," she says. "Aromatherapy is so much more than just a scented candle," Azzaro says. "If I can teach people about even one oil, then I'm doing my job."

There is probably no typical day for an aromatherapist, and there are many ways of treating clients. Some people incorporate aromatherapy with other holistic practices, such as massage or acupuncture. An aromatherapist meeting with a client for the first time takes his or her full medical history, including information about diet, lifestyle, emotional problems, and allergies. The aromatherapist may ask the client about his or her short- and long-term goals of treatment. The aromatherapist also checks for potential health risks, such an allergy either to inhaled or topical oils.

After ascertaining why the client is seeking help, the aromatherapist makes a blend of essential oils, often using these oils in a therapeutic massage. Aromatherapy oils can also be inhaled or used in a bath. Many aromatherapists also educate their clients and help them understand which oils and aromas they can use in their own home to further treatment.

Self-employed aromatherapists can set their own hours, working at times that best suit their clients. In addition to working in their own practices, many aromatherapists work at complementary therapy centers, spas, beauty therapy centers, nursing homes, and hospices.

Aromatherapists are registered with the Aromatherapy Registration Council, an independent organization that administers an examination for aromatherapists. Candidates must demonstrate a minimum level of knowledge about aromatherapy to pass the registration exam and earn the Registered Aromatherapist (R.A.) credential. After five years, aromatherapists must retake the exam.

Pitfalls

Many Americans don't know very much about aromatherapy, and therefore tend to be dismissive of this branch of complementary health care; some consider it ineffective. Self-employed therapists have to make their office hours around clients' needs, which may mean working evenings and weekends.

Perks

If you're interested in caring for other people in holistic ways, interacting with clients and helping them improve their lives, this is a great career for you.

Get a Jump on the Job

Read everything you can about aromatherapy and holistic health, and then visit an aromatherapist to learn more.

ART THERAPIST

OVERVIEW

Art therapy involves a lot more than asking a patient to interpret her own artwork. Rather, it's a kind of treatment based on the belief that the creative process involved in the making of art is healing and life-enhancing in and of itself. Art therapy is effective in helping to treat patients with problems in development, health, social skills, or mental health. Through creating art and talking about art with a patient, the therapist can help the patient cope with symptoms, stress, and traumatic experiences. An art therapist also can help the client better understand his or her problems and enjoy the life-affirming pleasures of artistic creativity.

Early in treatment with a client, the art therapist may ask the client to pick out collage pictures and make a self-portrait. Or the therapist might suggest the client create a piece of artwork to illustrate something the person is struggling with. Once the picture is completed, the art therapist is trained to ask specific kinds of questions to help clients talk about the artwork and explore what they created. The therapist probably would not say: "I'm going to tell you what it means that you drew a picture of yourself cowering in the corner under a black cloud." Instead, the therapist would be much more likely to ask: "Tell me about the picture you made" or "What do you notice first about this picture? Why?" The discussion becomes a springboard for deeper exploration into what might be bothering the client.

AT A GLANCE

Salary Range

Beginning therapists can earn about $25,000; average income ranges between $28,000 and $38,000, and top earning potential for salaried administrators ranges between $40,000 and $60,000, depending on location, the type of practice, and job responsibilities. Art therapists with doctoral degrees, state licensure, or who qualify in their state to conduct private practice have an earning potential of $75 to $90 an hour in private practice.

Education/Experience

Art therapists are trained in both art and therapy and hold a master's degree in art therapy or a related field. Undergraduate art therapy introductory courses and preparatory programs are offered in colleges across the country. Twenty-seven master's programs in art therapy have been approved by the American Art Therapy Association.

Personal Attributes

Sensitivity, insight, artistic talent, flexibility, a sense of humor, creativity, emotional stability, patience, and a capacity for insight into psychological processes. An art therapist must be an attentive listener, a keen observer, and be good with people.

Requirements

Art ability and training in art therapy are required. The educational, professional, and ethical standards for art therapists are regulated by the American Art Therapy Association. The Art Therapy Credentials Board (ATCB) is an independent organization that grants the Registered Art Therapist (ATR) credential after reviewing documentation of completed graduate education and postgraduate supervised experience. To qualify for the ATR credential, a person must complete the educational requirements and a minimum of 1,000 direct–client contact hours. One hour of supervision is required for every 10 hours of client contact. A registered art therapist can become board certified (ATR-BC) by passing a

(continues)

AT A GLANCE (continued)

written examination administered by the ATCB; the credential is maintained by completing continuing education credits.

Outlook

Art therapy is a growing profession and employment continues to increase as more and more professionals and clients recognize its value. Graduates of art therapy programs can find both full- and part-time jobs; those with A.T.R. and A.T.R.-BC credentials have a distinct advantage.

Art therapists work in facilities such as medical and psychiatric hospitals, outpatient facilities, clinics, residential treatment centers, halfway houses, shelters, schools, correctional facilities, elder care facilities, pain clinics, universities, and art studios. Typically, the art therapist works as part of a team of health care specialists, including doctors, psychologists, nurses, rehabilitation counselors, social workers, and teachers. Together, they determine and implement a client's program. Art therapists can also work as primary therapists in private practice.

Aimee Rozum, art therapist

Working as an artist and a counselor, Aimee Rozum never dreamed about combining her two interests until she saw an article about art therapy in the local newspaper. The article described a local university's program in clinical art therapy, and Rozum was hooked. "I was out of college and working in pastoral care," she says, "doing a lot of counseling. I was also an artist, and when I saw this field that put the two things together, a light bulb went off!"

Rozum explains that working with an art therapist is just one way to get treatment for personal problems. "Either clients go to an art therapist because they feel like working nonverbally," Rozum says, "or they are attracted to making art and feel that it's easier to express themselves nonverbally." Others get referred to an art therapist because working nonverbally is much more gentle, she says.

"It's easier to explore painful issues if you do it first by making imagery about it," she explains. While art therapists typically use art as a way of getting the patient to talk about problems, it's also sometimes possible to look at a piece of art and understand what a person's problems may be by what the images depict. Although nonverbal imagery is very individual, "if you've spent 10 years working with kids who are traumatized, you will notice general themes in the artwork by kids who are traumatized, sexually abused, or who have been in war situations."

If you're thinking about becoming an art therapist, Rozum recommends that you concentrate on studio art and psychology. "That's the background you have to have to get into a grad program," she says. "Look really closely at different grad programs, because they are very different from one another. It depends on what kind of art therapist you want to be."

For Rozum, the decision to combine art and therapy was the right one. "I love being an art therapist," she says. "It's a wonderful way to communicate with people. It's fun, it's not threatening, and people can become so shocked and surprised and impressed at the things they make. It's a wonderful thing, watching people discover things about themselves."

Art therapists work with all ages, from young children to elderly adults. They provide services to individuals, couples, families, groups, and communities. Art therapists are skilled in using a variety of media, including drawing, painting, clay, and ceramics, for treatment and assessment. These therapists also might conduct research as well as provide consultations to allied professionals.

Art therapists, who are trained in both art and therapy, understand human development, psychological theories, and clinical practice as well as artistic traditions, how to create art, and the healing potential of art. In their daily sessions, art therapists use art to help assess and treat mental illnesses. For example, the therapist may ask a client to create a picture about how the person is feeling at that moment and then discusses why the client chose to create that particular bit of art.

Art therapists use a variety of artistic media with a patient as a way of learning more about the person's development, personality, interests, problems, and worries. Using art, a trained art therapist can help patients work through emotional conflicts, learn more about themselves, develop better social skills, manage problem behaviors, solve problems, lessen anxiety, and increase self-esteem.

Art therapy as a separate field developed simultaneously in England and the United States, emerging as a distinct profession in the 1930s. At the beginning of the 20th century, psychiatrists became interested in the art work done by patients and studied it to see if there was a link between the art and the illness of their patients. Since then, the profession of art therapy has grown into an effective and important method of communication, assessment, and treatment with many populations. Most art therapists work in clinic situations, hospices, nursing homes, community mental health centers, community art programs, and schools.

Grounded in theories from both psychoanalysis and art education, most art therapists find that they draw from both approaches, modifying what they do or emphasize according to the person with whom they're working. Experts don't agree whether patients improve because of their discussions about a work of art or because of the specific act of creating a piece of art, but whatever is happening, art does seem to help people better understand their problems.

Pitfalls

Jobs in the field can be tough to find. Because of health insurance regulations, you can't work in any kind of institution with just an art therapy degree—you must also have a state counseling license.

Perks

If you love art and helping others, this is a great way to combine the two in a career.

Get a Jump on the Job

Take as many art classes as you can in high school, plus any psychology courses your school may offer. This will prepare you well for a major in art therapy once you get to college. Read more about art therapy by researching it on the Web or consulting the books listed in Read More About It at the end of this book.

ASTRONAUT

OVERVIEW

When the U.S. space program began in 1959, there were only seven astronauts in the entire country, all of whom had been in the armed forces. A lot has changed in the program since then.

Today astronauts (derived from Greek words meaning *star sailor*) include Americans from every race, creed, color, and gender. From thousands of applications from all over the world, every two years a wide cross section of America—100 men and women—are chosen to begin an intensive astronaut candidate training program.

Every two years, scientists from many different fields go to the Johnson Space Center in Houston, Texas, to train for a year or two in the hopes of being chosen as a member of a space shuttle crew—and then return to their original jobs. Some get to fly into space, and some do not. Along the way, they got up really early and worked late into the night, pushing themselves to get ready to be called at any moment for a potential space mission. The ability to work long hours under intense pressure comes in handy during space flight, when scientists pack as many experiments as possible into the hours they have.

Your quest to become an astronaut begins after you've got all the degrees and qualifications you think you'll need, along with some great research or internships under your belt. Then it's time to submit U.S. government application form #171 to the Johnson Space Center in Houston. Officials there will rank your application

AT A GLANCE

Salary Range

$40,000 (GS-11) to $82,000 (GS-14); each individual's past experience and achievements play a part in determination of the starting salary.

Education/Experience

The minimum degree requirement for an astronaut is a bachelor's degree from an accredited institution, followed by three years of related, increasingly responsible professional experience. Most astronauts, however, have received postgraduate degrees in chemistry, physics, medicine, biology, aerospace engineering, or math and can substitute education for all or part of their work experience requirement.

Personal Attributes

Being able to work as a team player; adaptability; the ability to focus; appreciation of ethnic, cultural and American history.

Requirements

Excellent oral and written communication skills; excellent grades and science/math skills, along with sterling recommendations from top-notch professors who know your work. Being bilingual is a plus, especially if one day you'll be working at an international space station. You must be between 5'4" and 6'4" to be a pilot and between 4'10½" and 6'4" inches to be a mission specialist. You also need to be in top physical condition to pass the requisite NASA physical.

Outlook

Poor. Every two years, only 20 astronauts are hired out of more than 4,000 applicants.

according to height and your specialty. After the first round, the applications are then scrutinized further by tougher requirements. The 118 remaining applicants are invited to Houston to undergo a week of interviews, medical exams, and orientation. Once selected, candidates begin a rigorous training program.

If you want to be an astronaut pilot, you'll need to have logged at least 1,000 hours of flight time in command of a jet air-

Scott Kelly, space shuttle commander

As a kid, Scott Kelly dreamed of many different careers: baseball player, race car driver, doctor, test pilot, astronaut. Eventually, his interests took him to the New York Maritime College, where he earned a B.S. in electrical engineering in 1987. After joining the Navy and becoming a test pilot, he earned an M.S. in aviation systems from the University of Tennessee in 1996.

Selected by NASA in 1996—along with his twin brother, Mark, who was also a pilot—Kelly reported to the Johnson Space Center. Three years later, after completing his training, he served as commander on STS-103, an eight-day mission to install new instruments and upgrade systems on the Hubble space telescope. Next, he served as NASA's Director of Operations in Star City, Russia, and served as a backup crew member for ISS Expedition-5. As current Space Station Branch Chief within the Astronaut Office, he'll be commanding an assembly mission to the International Space Station scheduled to launch in 2007.

What many people don't realize is that being a NASA astronaut doesn't mean you're constantly flying into outer space. In between spending time on the shuttles, there's lots of work to be done on the ground. "You have jobs within the astronaut office, to support the different programs we're involved in," Kelly says, "and to work on missions that will fly in the future. I've been here 10 years, and I've flown once. I'll probably fly a second time next year, and then maybe a third flight." In fact, that's the downside of being an astronaut, he says—"not getting to fly as much as I'd like." Three flights in 16 years is about average for NASA astronauts. Four flights in total is about typical for an astronaut's career.

If you are good in science and you'd love the chance to work for NASA, you'll need to start out by focusing on some type of technical career. "My advice would be to choose a career field in something that NASA considers qualifying," Kelly says, "such as science, engineering, math, physics." It's also important to choose something you generally enjoy doing, Kelly says. "If you choose something you like, you're more likely to do well in it. NASA wants people who have done well in previous careers." But he wouldn't advise trying for a career as a Navy pilot or Air Force pilot just to become an astronaut. Instead, he says, you should choose a career that you're interested in for its own sake.

"It's also important to be a well-rounded person, not someone like theoretical physicists who haven't proven they can do something, [but someone who is] operationally oriented, like flying airplanes or operating sophisticated systems."

The best part of his job is that there's always something different going on, he says. "It's doing a job that's very hands on, that's very varied in scope. It's interesting—and certainly the flying-in-space part is great, but that doesn't happen very often."

When it does happen, it's not something he'll easily forget. "Being in space is probably the most exciting thing you can do," he says. "It's very exciting, very challenging."

craft before you're even considered. With few exceptions, most of the current and former pilot positions have been filled by men who have served or who are currently active in the U.S. Armed Forces. During training all crew members train aboard a T-38 jet because its controls are exactly the same as those in the space shuttle.

Pitfalls

The work can be long and difficult, and long hours are common. This is also a hazardous, high-risk occupation. Once you're hired to train for missions, you're committing yourself to a training period of one to two years in Houston. If you're chosen as an astronaut you'll be expected to stay with NASA for at least five years, without a guarantee that you'll ever go into space. Training is intense and often in low-gravity conditions, including land and sea survival training and scuba diving.

Perks

If space is the final frontier, astronauts are the last of the great pioneers. Can you imagine looking out a cockpit window and seeing planet Earth spinning beneath you?

It's a sight few people have ever had, but those who have experienced it say it's a life-changing moment.

Get a Jump on the Job

Math and science are the keys to a career as an astronaut, so spend as much time as possible studying those subjects. Read everything you can get your hands on about astronauts and space. And because 64 percent of astronauts have been scouts, you might want to consider getting involved in scouting. When getting ready to choose a college, note that NASA contributes money to 51 colleges through its Space Grant Consortia. By attending one of these schools, you'll know that the curricula will match NASA guidelines. (To receive a list of the consortia schools, write to: NASA Education Division, Code FEO2, 300 E Street S.W., Washington, D.C. 20546.)

Also, if you're aiming for an astronaut career, as soon as you get on campus you should go check out the possibility of a NASA internship to get experience; don't wait until your senior year to miss this chance.

ASTRONOMER

OVERVIEW

The quintessential astronomer, Dr. Carl Sagan managed to capture the public's fascination with all things extraterrestrial and triggered a stampede of young astronomers into the field.

Astronomy, which is sometimes considered a subfield of physics, uses the principles of mathematics and physics to explore the nature of the universe. It includes the study of galaxies, the sun, moon, stars, and planets. As an astronomer, you may concentrate on different aspects of the field, such as the origin and evolution of stars, solar astronomy, the formation of galaxies, or planetary science. Other astronomers apply their expertise to areas such as space flight, satellite communication, and navigation. Some astronomers design and use programs that require direct observation of the skies, while others (called *theorists*) use computer models to try to solve problems concerning the structure and evolution of the sun, moon, stars, planets, and galaxies.

Astronomers work in observatories, university laboratories, research centers, and planetariums. Although we tend to think of astronomers as permanently connected to their telescopes, gazing up into the heavens, there is much more to the job. When an astronomer makes an observation, the data must be recorded and then carefully analyzed.

Because most astronomers teach at colleges and universities, they must spend a great deal of their time preparing for class. Most universities expect their professors to conduct research and get their results

AT A GLANCE

Salary Range

A typical salary for a beginning astronomer is between $30,000 and $40,000 a year. Experienced astronomers with a large body of research may earn upwards of $75,000.

Education/Experience

Most astronomers in the United States have a Ph.D. in astronomy or physics. There are about 180 colleges and universities in the United States that offer Ph.D. degrees in physics and about 40 that offer a Ph.D. in astronomy.

Personal Attributes

You should be inquisitive and observant, with the ability to analyze and make sense out of what you observe. Most astronomers are very good at math, and are logical and practical. Because one research project can last for years, it's important to be persistent and patient. You should be able to clearly communicate the results of your studies and research, so good writing and speaking skills are important.

Requirements

Most astronomers teach at colleges and universities. Getting and keeping a teaching job may entail research and publication requirements, as well as security clearances. Other types of astronomy jobs, such as with a museum or private institution, may also require security clearances.

Outlook

Unfortunately, there aren't many astronomy jobs, and not much hope that many more will appear any time soon. The number of jobs is extremely limited, and people who have earned their Ph.D.s and are hoping to become astronomers may have to take jobs in other areas while they wait for an astronomy job.

published, so astronomers also spend a lot of time researching and writing reports.

In addition, they may have to apply for grants for equipment or funding for their research, spend time traveling to meetings, speaking before groups, reviewing proposals, and developing new instruments and observation techniques. Most astronomers would prefer to have more time to be with their telescopes, but they understand that the job entails these other duties as well.

Pitfalls

Because you need a Ph.D. to get a job as a professional astronomer, you'll need to spend a lot of time getting that degree: It

Dr. Jeremy Mould, astronomer

As an observational astronomer, Dr. Jeremy Mould spends much of his time trying to figure out the evolution of the stars and the distance of the galaxies. He's also the director of the National Optical Astronomy Observatory (NOAO) near Tucson, a group of observatories that attracts astronomers from all over the world to access the powerful telescopes and research opportunities. Although he enjoys running NOAO, his passion is using the telescopes and analyzing his results to try to determine the story of the universe.

"Most current stellar population studies are tied to the star formation history of galaxies," Mould explains. "You can study it locally within the Milky Way, or you can study it by looking further back in time, beyond our galaxy. Both approaches require large telescopes and the ability to resolve distant objects with great precision, and both are part of astronomy's major theme of telling the story of the universe from the big bang to present day."

In short, Mould says, he tries to figure out what it's all about. "Discovering the universe's secrets is extremely rewarding—and difficult!" he says.

Born in Bristol, England, Mould moved to Australia when he was 14. While he was studying science and physics at the University of Melbourne, he became interested in astronomy. He went on to earn a Ph.D. in astronomy and physics from the Australian National University in Canberra.

In addition to his work with NOAO, Mould has served as one of three principal investigators for a Hubble Space Telescope Key Project team. Using information gathered by the Hubble telescope, the team's job was to measure the expansion rate of the universe within a 10 percent degree of accuracy. He also has worked on NASA projects, where he is a member of its space science advisory committee.

Mould advises students interested in becoming an astronomer to sign up for all the math and science courses they can possibly take. "Studying physics and mathematics is the best preparation for many careers in science, but especially astronomy," Mould says. "Then follow up on whatever it is that interests you the most."

can take as much as six years after you earn your undergraduate degree to complete a Ph.D. in astronomy or physics. There are only about 40 U.S. schools that offer Ph.D. degrees in astronomy, so getting accepted into an astronomy graduate program can be difficult. In addition, jobs are quite scarce and competition for them is tough. Astronomers don't earn as much money as scientists in some other fields, such as biomedicine or biophysics.

Perks

If you're fascinated by the heavens and all that they contain, what better job could you imagine than being an astronomer? Many people experience an almost mystical sense of awe as they study the sky. Because most astronomers teach as well as conduct research, their jobs are varied and interesting.

Get a Jump on the Job

Take as much math and science as you can (especially calculus, chemistry, and physics) and work hard at it so you get the best grades possible. Make sure well before your senior year that you've chosen all the courses you'll need to be admitted to an astronomy program. Hone your writing skills and make sure you're proficient on the computer. Visit an observatory to get an idea of how they're run, and read all you can about astronomy and space.

CRIME SCENE EXAMINER

OVERVIEW

If your image of a crime scene examiner is based on TV shows such as *CSI* or *Law and Order*, here are the facts: First, it's extremely rare in real police work to have evidence fall together the way it does on TV shows. Second, the same person or team doesn't handle a crime from the time it's reported until it's solved. In reality, investigation duties are divided and assigned to different members of a police department or other law enforcement agency. One piece of that larger effort is examination of the crime scene.

Crime scene examiners examine and analyze crime scenes. They collect evidence, come up with theories as to what occurred, and record exactly what the crime scene was like when they encountered it. They take photographs, do DNA sampling, dust for fingerprints, identify potential clues, and otherwise process the scene. Investigating a crime scene is slow, methodical work that requires the complete attention of the examiner. After all, anything in that scene could be a potential clue. Being able to recognize a potential clue can mean the difference between solving and not solving the crime.

Crime scene examiners are expected to be able to recognize tire track and shoe print evidence, collect evidence for hair or fiber testing, and test for latent bloodstains. While some crime scene examiners also process evidence in the laboratory,

AT A GLANCE

Salary Range

Average salary ranges from $32,300 to $53,500, depending on location, experience, educational background, and other factors.

Education/Experience

Not all police departments or agencies require a college degree in order to be a crime scene examiner, but having at least an undergraduate degree is becoming increasingly preferred. You'll need a high school diploma at the very least. Because examining crime scenes requires a mixture of law enforcement and scientific knowledge, a bachelor's degree in either criminal justice with a concentration in natural science, or a natural science degree with concentration in law enforcement, is recommended.

Personal Attributes

Any sort of work in law enforcement requires that the candidate be honest, able to make sound decisions quickly, and able to communicate well with colleagues and the public. A crime scene examiner has to be able to withstand some very unpleasant situations. You must be flexible, able to think and react quickly, and have the ability to recognize and pay close attention to detail.

Requirements

Many crime scene examiner jobs are subject to civil service regulations, which require candidates to be at least 20 years old and able to meet certain physical and personal qualifications. It's likely that you'll be required to undergo physical exams that include vision and hearing screenings and tests for strength, endurance, and agility. Background checks are conducted and those with a criminal record are not eligible. You might be subject to lie detector tests and probably will be required to undergo drug testing before and during your employment. Crime scene examiners undergo a period of training before they begin the job and are likely to be required to complete continuing education courses while on the job.

AT A GLANCE

Outlook

Good. Jobs in law enforcement are expected to increase by between 21 and 35 percent through 2012. As our society becomes more security conscious, there will be good opportunities for people looking for work in this area.

most larger police departments work primarily in the field, while criminalists work with evidence in the laboratory.

Crime scene examiners, however, must do a fair amount of paperwork to document what they've learned from the scene and often must prepare for and testify in court.

Pitfalls

Crime scene examiners encounter some pretty gruesome scenes and circumstances on a regular basis. When crime scene examiners are on call, they have to be ready to report to the scene of the crime at any hour of the night or day.

Perks

Crime scene examiners are by no means the highest paid people in the criminal justice field, but studies show that very few crime scene examiners voluntarily leave their jobs for other positions. This indicates a high degree of job satisfaction.

Terri Carter, crime scene examiner

If there's an arson, an armed robbery, an assault, or a murder, Terri Carter is there. She has worked for the Palm Bay, Florida, police department for 20 years—the last seven of which she's been a crime scene examiner. Prior to that, she worked in the department's criminal investigation bureau.

While most people think of crime scenes primarily as places where homicides have occurred, murder is only one of the many crimes Carter helps to solve. She responds to calls for burglary in homes and businesses, armed robbery, carjackings, arson, aggravated assault, sexual assault, home invasion, child abuse, elder abuse, suicide, suspicious deaths, traffic fatalities, shootings, knifings, and other serious crimes.

Carter works 40 hours a week and is on call for one week out of every three. That means she's responsible for responding to a crime scene at any hour of the day or night, including weekends. She's usually at the crime scene by herself, except in the case of a homicide or other very serious or extensive crime, when a team will be assigned to work at the scene.

When she's not working in the field at a crime scene, Carter spends much of her time completing paperwork at her desk. Crime scene evidence needs to be carefully documented and reported, since incorrect reporting could make the evidence invalid and worthless. She helps with some of the processing of evidence in the department's small laboratory. Other evidence is sent to a larger crime lab for processing. She also spends a considerable amount of time preparing reports for the courts and testifying at court trials.

(continues)

(continued)

Carter has young children, which makes being on call inconvenient and sometimes means she misses events and activities in which her children are participating. That can be stressful, she says, but she understands that being on call is part of the job and she works at making the best of it.

Carter started out working in the records department for the Palm Bay Police Department and she's still working toward a college degree. Over the years, however, she's managed to complete courses offered by many agencies, such as the Federal Bureau of Investigation, the Florida Department of Law Enforcement, the Miami/Dade Metropolitan Police Institute, and the Bureau of Alcohol, Tobacco, Firearms and Explosives.

"Because crime scene technology changes so rapidly, there's a real need for continuing education," Carter says. She's taken courses in crime scene photography, advanced crime scene processing, homicide investigations, latent fingerprint processing, forensic evidence collection, firearms training, and child injury and death investigations.

Examining crime scenes isn't an easy job, and it's certainly not for everyone, Carter says. "Some of the calls can be difficult to deal with, as you can imagine," she says. "And being on call so much is difficult, especially with the kids." Crime is generally unpleasant, and crime scene examiners are exposed on a regular basis to sights and situations that can be extremely disturbing. All in all, however, Carter thinks it's worth it.

"I love my job," she said. "It's very challenging and it's very rewarding. I do something different every day, which keeps the job really interesting. I really can't imagine doing anything else."

Most crime scene examiners like the fact that every day and every case is different, and that there is great variety in the work. Most people who work in any aspect of law enforcement are committed to public safety and public service and find satisfaction in working to make their communities safer and more appealing.

Get a Jump on the Job

Begin reading about crime scene investigation to become more familiar with the work. Many community colleges offer criminal justice classes, including crime scene investigation. Some high schools work in partnership with community colleges to allow high school students to take college courses. Ask your guidance counselor if your school district participates in such a program. The best way to find out more about being a crime scene examiner is to talk with someone who does the job. You could call your local police department, explain that you're interested in crime scene examination as a career, and ask if it would be possible for you to speak with someone in that position.

CRIMINOLOGIST

OVERVIEW

If you can't get enough of TV police procedurals, gobble up mysteries, and are fascinated by the criminal mind, you might enjoy working in the field of criminology. It's a field with many choices, ranging from local police officer to international security consultant. In general, however, criminologists study social behavior. They look at what's considered "normal" and then study factors that can cause people to deviate from normal. Criminologists also try to understand why crime occurs, how it occurs, and how it can be prevented. They may deal with statistics, study society's attitudes toward criminals, analyze factors that contribute to criminal behavior, interpret social trends linked to crime, and give advice on government policy about crime.

If you think the field of criminology could be for you, you might consider being a college or university professor, police officer, FBI agent, state medical examiner, liquor control officer, crime scene investigator, private detective, security consultant, civilian investigator for the military, federal judge, and one of many other careers.

The federal government contains more than 80 agencies with law enforcement capabilities, including the FBI, CIA, Secret Service, Postal Service, and Bureau of Alcohol, Tobacco, Firearms and Explosives. Thousands of people work as background investigators for the federal government, performing background checks on others hoping to get government jobs. The Department of the Interior hires 90 special agent wildlife officers who work in national parks to prevent people from poaching, bringing animals into the country illegally, or committing other illegal acts. Every state has agencies with law enforcement capabilities.

AT A GLANCE

Salary Range

Salaries for criminologists range between $32,270 and $66,460, according to All Criminal Justice Schools, an online directory of criminal justice education and careers.

Education/Experience

Because so many jobs fall under the umbrella of criminology, there are many different educational paths available. Criminologists who want to teach at the university level will need at least a master's degree, and more likely a Ph.D. Other jobs in criminology require only a bachelor's degree.

Personal Attributes

A criminologist should have an innate understanding of human nature and how people react in various circumstances. You must be able to see the big picture but be detail oriented as well. You should be able to think logically, behave responsibly, and demonstrate creativity and an ability to think outside the box. Criminologists must be excellent communicators both verbally and in writing.

Requirements

Most jobs in criminology will require security clearances, background checks, and drug tests. Because there are such a range of jobs in the field of criminology, requirements will vary greatly. Some states require that criminologists take written exams and be licensed.

Outlook

Jobs in the area of criminology are expected to increase at a rate that is higher than average through 2012.

There also are many opportunities for jobs in criminology in the private sector, from investigating cases of insurance fraud to providing security services to a corporation.

Many criminologists enter the field in one area and end up someplace completely different. For instance, some criminologists working as police officers become very interested in the legal aspects of the field and decide to pursue law degrees. They may end up as lawyers or judges. Other criminologists may cross over from jobs in the private sector to the public sector, or the other way around.

While there are many opportunities in the area of criminology, the field demands high-caliber candidates. You'll need to get a well-rounded education, and, in many cases, be willing to pursue advanced degrees. You should have knowledge of a range of subject areas, including psychology, communications, sociology, mathematics, history, and geography. There are lots of jobs in criminology, but it's a competitive field that demands intelligent, responsible individuals.

Pitfalls

Depending on the job you're looking at, you might have to commit to a long educational endeavor. Competition for some jobs is very tight. Some criminology jobs, such as police officer and federal agent can be dangerous, which can cause a great deal of stress. Professionals in some areas of

Robert Mutchnick, criminologist

Robert Mutchnick is a criminology professor at Indiana University of Pennsylvania, a school with a reputation for an excellent criminology program. He has spent 30 years teaching criminology and has found every minute of it fascinating. "I never get tired of it, that's for sure," Mutchnick says. "There's always something going on that keeps it interesting."

To Mutchnick, who has an undergraduate degree in sociology and a Ph.D. in criminology, it was always the teaching part of criminology that interested him the most. "I always wanted to be an academician," he says. "I like the life." And for anyone who might be considering teaching, there are still good opportunities available at hundreds of criminal justice programs across the country that need teachers.

Anyone interested in criminology should work hard to get into a good college and build a good educational foundation, Mutchnick advises, noting that it's particularly important to be able to write well, because you're going to have to be able to express your thoughts and observations. Because criminology is such as broad field with so many different opportunities, Mutchnick suggested that you take some time to explore the various jobs and careers available. "Try to get a feel for the system and what part of the system interests you the most," he advised.

However, Mutchnick warned, potential criminologists should be aware that real-life criminology is much different than what you might have seen on a television show such as *CSI: Crime Scene Investigation.*

"Most kids now are watching *CSI* and thinking that that's the kind of work they want to do," Mutchnick said. "But that's misleading. That's not what criminology is like. You need to be realistic and find out what the field is really like."

criminology have high rates of depression, emotional problems, and even suicide.

Perks

Criminology is a fascinating field that is constantly changing. A criminologist never runs out of material from which to learn. And, because so many jobs fall under the umbrella of criminology, you can move around within the field if you think a different job would be a better fit.

Get a Jump on the Job

An increasing number of colleges and universities offer summer courses or camps for high school students that deal with different areas of criminology. You could look into getting a part-time job that relates to criminology, such as a police dispatcher. Read everything you can find about the various jobs found within the field of criminology and take an interdisciplinary approach to academics, leaning toward the liberal arts.

CRYONICS RESEARCHER

OVERVIEW

Cryonics is the science of using ultra-cold liquid temperature to preserve the whole body, head, or brain of a person recently declared legally dead, in the hope that the person might be restored to good health at some time in the future when technology becomes available to do so. A patient held in such a state is said to be in "cryonic suspension." The word *cryonics* is derived from *cryogenics*, the physical science of very low temperatures.

Cryonics—a somewhat controversial branch of science—is called a "speculative life support technology," according to cryonics experts. It's based on the hope that in the future, doctors will be able to heal at the cellular and molecular levels.

Cryonics is not a fancy alternative to burial or other mortuary practice, nor is it a way of preserving dead tissue. Just as organ donation involves the recovery of living organs from a donor who is brain dead, cryonics involves stabilizing the viable brain of a patient who is legally deceased because the heart has stopped. However, cryonics cannot be used to preserve anyone who is truly brain dead. At the same time, it is not legally possible to cryonically suspend patients *before* they are legally dead. Although cryonics researchers believe it would be better to cool a patient before illness causes so much physical damage that it results in death, it's not presently allowed by law, even for someone in great suffering or with a terminal illness.

While cryonics is still controversial, more and more respected mainstream scientists, researchers, and doctors have been researching ways to revive a person safely from cryonic suspension, despite damage from old age, disease, accident, and the freezing process itself. Research is especially active in the field of nanotechnology (the manipulation of individual atoms or molecules to build or repair virtually any physical object, including human cells and biological tissue).

You may be surprised to learn that it's a myth that "brain death" occurs after only a few minutes without oxygen. The basic health of a brain in the first minutes and even hours after the heart stops is surprisingly good. It's the restoration of warm blood circulation to an injured brain that causes devastating destruction. "Absolute" death may only be said to occur when the brain's essential information is destroyed—and brain preservation is precisely what cryonic suspension aims to achieve. Brain death actually refers to an irreversible loss of all activity of the entire brain, including the brain stem, in a patient on life support. It's true that a patient who doesn't get enough oxygen at normal body temperature for many minutes, and who is then revived, will probably be diagnosed as brain dead the next day. But that's not because the brain "died" without oxygen. It would be more accurate, cryobiologists explain, to say the brain died during resuscitation because there was no way to stop the injured brain from self-destructing in the hours after resuscitation.

Sergey Sheleg, M.D., Ph.D., cryonics researcher

Born in Belarus, a small country near Poland that was once part of the former Soviet Union, Dr. Sergey Sheleg has been fascinated for all of his professional life with the brain and with neuroscience. As senior research scientist at Alcor Life Extension Foundation, his job is to design techniques related to cryonics and the best ways to prevent brain damage during initial perfusion (passage of fluid through tissue). Alcor, a nonprofit organization founded in 1972, is the world leader in cryonics, cryonics research, and cryonics technology.

Dr. Sheleg received his M.D. in Belarus in 1994, and his Ph.D. in neuro-oncology eight years later. Once in the United States, he worked in various postdoctoral fellowships at the National Institutes of Health and at the U.S. Food and Drug Administration, moving to Alcor in 2005 to continue to work on the problems of brain microcirculation. "In cryobiology," he says, "all of these topics are related to my previous research."

It's an area of research that's still quite new. "There were not too many specialists in the world who worked on the problem," he says, "just one in Germany, one in America. I worked on the problem in Belarus to try to devise a method to improve microcirculation in the brain in the hope that technology can improve the results after CPR."

After reading about cryonics more than 10 years ago, he was fascinated with the research possibilities. "All my research work is related to neuroscience," he says. "At NIH, I did experiments into the malignant transformation of the brain cells. In my country, my research was related to neuro-oncology and to local chemotherapy of malignant brain tumors."

It's a field that he still finds fascinating. "Neuroscience is extremely exciting," he says. "There are so many interesting problems, like the problems of brain death, psychiatry, neurochemistry. There are so many things that can be discovered in the future."

Young people who are interested in neuroscience and cryobiology will have fascinating research to conduct, he says. "The researchers who are doing the research will help to solve so many problems in the near and far future."

If you think that cryonics research sounds interesting, there are basically two tracks you can follow—either studying medicine, or engineering. Paramedics, perfusionists, nurses, and physicians can all find work in this field. Cryonics companies hire these professionals on either a full-time or contract basis. Scientists and engineers develop cryonics procedures and build specialized equipment to implement them.

Pitfalls

Any student contemplating a career in cryobiology (the study of life at low temperatures) should be aware that cryonics is a highly controversial subject. It is not always socially acceptable, and discussions of this work may make some individuals uncomfortable.

Perks

If science is your cup of tea, there can be few jobs more exciting than extending the frontiers of knowledge in the realm of neuroscience. Ultimately, any research breakthroughs you find will have implications not just for cryonics but for modern medicine as well.

Get a Jump on the Job

If cryonics fascinates you, you should study lots of chemistry, biology, and math in high school and plan on majoring in pre-med or engineering. Participate in science fairs or science camps if research is something you'd enjoy. Volunteer at a local hospital to get a feel for the atmosphere, and see what you can pick up.

CRYPTOGRAPHER

OVERVIEW

If you have an excellent head for figures and enjoy puzzles, the burgeoning field of information security—from making and breaking codes to developing software security systems—may be for you.

Cryptology is an umbrella term for cryptography and cryptanalysis and is considered to be an unusual branch of engineering. Cryptography is concerned with linguistic and mathematical techniques used to disguise communications. The study of how to circumvent the use of cryptography is called *cryptanalysis* (code breaking). In practice, the term *cryptography* is often used to refer to the field as a whole. No matter what you call it, however, it's a relatively tough field to enter, and you've got to be a crack mathematician in order to excel here. Opportunities are opening up in information security, as well as designing and implementing secure operating procedures.

Historically, cryptography was concerned solely with encryption (converting information from its normal understandable form into an unreadable format requiring secret knowledge to decode). Encryption was used mostly to protect classified communications by spies, military leaders, and diplomats. However, modern cryptography involves more than just keeping secrets; it's used for everything from authenticating digital signatures to electronic voting and digital cash.

Cryptographic technology is also an important part of computing and telecommunications. While older forms of cryptography were concerned with language

AT A GLANCE

Salary Range

From $38,930 to more than $112,780, with the average between $56,160 and $112,780. Salaries depend on where you are employed: For academics and those in the public sector, salaries are comparatively low, but in the private sector salaries rival those for management consultants.

Education/Experience

Most have at least a bachelor's degree in mathematics or computer science, plus graduate degrees in mathematics. There are few formal qualifications available in the cryptological field, but an increasing number of institutions are offering further courses. Postgraduate work at the Ph.D. level is usually required for cryptanalysts working in research or teaching at the university level.

Personal Attributes

Naturally curious, with a penchant for creating and breaking cryptograms and difficult codes; talent for math and computer science; logical problem-solvers with a great deal of patience and mental stamina. Cryptographers need communication skills and should enjoy working independently and synthesizing information. They tackle problems without losing heart, stubbornly working through possible solutions.

Requirements

All cryptographers must be well educated with a good background in mathematics, computer science, economics, and English.

Outlook

The world of the cryptographer is an international one, and there are opportunities internationally, both in academia and the private sector. All storage solution software, compression solution software, and authentication packages use some sort of an encryption, and the companies producing these products are always looking for bright minds to strengthen their software. Financial industry software companies in particular hire people with a cryptographic background.

Arjen Lenstra, cryptographer

In the exotic world of international cryptography, Arjen Lenstra is a world-renowned expert in evaluating, designing, and developing the cryptographic algorithms that protect sensitive information as it's communicated electronically. He's spent his career working, teaching, and consulting at a number of well-known places such as IBM and the University of Chicago. Today, he works for Bell Labs' Computing Sciences Research Center, the research division of Lucent Technologies.

Dr. Lenstra's formal training is in computational number theory—a field concerned with finding and implementing efficient computer algorithms for solving various problems rooted in number theory. He holds a bachelor's degree in mathematics and physics, a master's degree in mathematics, and a doctorate in mathematics and computer science from the University of Amsterdam.

He got started in the cryptography field when he was working on a particular mathematical problem of great interest to cryptographers. "They became very much interested in my work," he says, "and invited me to their meetings." Gradually, the cryptographers pulled him into their specialty area. "Because it's a fun field," he says, "I stayed there."

To Lenstra, cryptography is an exciting, lively field where "new results may from one day to the next turn everything upside down, with potentially worldwide impact," he explains. He specializes in the security of systems that are widely used in e-commerce applications, such as how electronic transactions are secured. He also evaluates encryption systems used in e-commerce. Dr. Lenstra focuses on how academic cryptologic research and computational number theory affect practical security practices. He believes that bridging the gap between what's theoretically possible and what's practical is a major research challenge.

Code breaking is Dr. Lenstra's favorite activity, but he admits it's on the technical side. "Simply put, one of my favorite subjects is integer factorization, such as finding the factors 3

---

patterns, more recently it has emphasized the use of mathematics, including number theory, information theory, and statistics.

If you were to guess who's hiring cryptographers, you'd probably say the CIA and all those other clandestine governmental agencies concerned with spies and national defense. But they're by no means the only people interested in cryptography. For example, cryptographers are required by most large companies, such as Hewlett-Packard, which has its own in-house information security team. Cable TV companies, who encode their signals before sending them out, are interested in cryptography, as is the entire financial industry, which uses cryptography with their automated teller machines, which communicate with banks via encoded radio signals that change for each transaction. You'll also find cryptologists working for universities, insurance companies, scientific institutions, research agencies, telecommunications companies, computer design firms, consulting firms, and science and engineering firms.

Pitfalls

Although cryptographers usually work in a comfy office environment in front of a computer, long hours and knotty problems

or 5 of the composite integer 15." That's a straightforward example, he says, pointing out that 15 is easy to factor. "But if the number to be factored has hundreds of digits and two unknown prime factors of hundreds of digits each, it looks like a very tough problem." The difficulty of that problem underlies many security protocols used on the Internet by banks, the military, and the government, he says. "But no one knows for sure if it really is difficult." It would still be possible that someone could suddenly figure out an easy way to solve the problem, he says, with devastating effects for security applications. "Part of my work is trying to figure out how hard that problem of integer factorization is."

Dr. Lenstra advises budding cryptographers to first study math for a few years and cover the basics. The earlier you start and become completely familiar with complicated mathematical techniques, he explains, the better your chances of survival in the highly competitive, challenging, and exciting world of cryptography. "Then pick up and read the few basic textbooks on crypto and do the exercises. No doubt you will find a problem that you will like working on. There are plenty! Both in cryptanalysis (code breaking) and cryptography (designing new codes), there are lots and lots of wide open problems."

Part of the attraction of the field of cryptography is the worldwide cryptographic community, which includes about a thousand researchers scattered across the globe. "It's like a big group of friends," he says. "Wherever you go, you will run into someone whom you know from one of the field's three big annual meetings.

"The potential of surprises is what I like best, from a scientific point of view. It is also what I like least about the field, from a business point of view. If you like guaranteed stability, cryptography is not for you. If you like flexibility, inventiveness, and meeting some of the smartest people around, it is great!"

aren't uncommon, especially when near deadlines.

Perks

If numbers fascinate you, few jobs are more exciting than the number crunching involved in a cryptographer's career. Linked to security systems of banks and computers, it's a lively, growing field.

Get a Jump on the Job

If you've got a yen for puzzles, mathematical conundrums, and secret or hidden messages of all kinds, start early by taking every math course you can in high school. Read up on cryptology and practice with encryption and decryption by reading books and making your own codes, every chance you get.

DOCUMENT EXAMINER

OVERVIEW

If you love to watch television cop shows, mystery series, or Court TV, you probably know all about document examiners—the experts who can offer an opinion about the legal status of everything from Grandpa's will to that anonymous ransom note cobbled together from yesterday's newspaper.

But there's still some confusion about the different types of document examiners, and what they all do. A document examiner is a specialist focusing on ink, paper, and typewriter identification. Forensic document examiners offer written opinions on disputed document problems such as wills, deeds, medical records, income tax records, time sheets, contracts, loan agreements, election petitions, checks, and anonymous letters. Qualified forensic document examiners often testify as experts in both criminal and civil trials in federal, state, and local courts as well as administrative hearings.

A handwriting analyst specializes in identifying personality traits for various areas including business needs, counseling, compatibility, and job assessments; a handwriting expert specializes in forensics, and can identify signatures and other writings to determine whether they are forgeries, or whether they're valid for the stated purposes.

Handwriting analysis is the study of printing and cursive writing to determine a person's personality traits. It can be used to produce a personality profile for

AT A GLANCE

Salary Range
$50 to $500 per analysis.

Education/Experience
There is no college degree or major in document examination, but you can be certified in this field via short courses or correspondence courses. Most document examiners have undergraduate or master's degrees in criminal justice or forensic science; most regional and national forensic science organizations require a degree as a condition of membership.

Personal Attributes
Patience and attention to detail. You must be able to see the big picture but be detail oriented as well. Document examiners and handwriting experts must be excellent communicators and be able to express themselves both verbally and in writing because some jobs may involve court testimony.

Requirements
There are no federal licensure requirements for handwriting experts or document examiners. However, document examiners can be certified by the American Board of Forensic Document Examiners (ABFDE). Minimum qualifications for certification are an undergraduate degree, two years of full-time training in a recognized document laboratory, and full-time practice of forensic document examination. Training should include the study of all aspects of questioned documents and expertise is gained only with the examination of thousands of documents in a variety of cases. Organized in 1977, at present the ABFDE certifies less than 200 active examiners within the United States and Canada.

Outlook
Jobs in the area of document examination are expected to remain steady through 2012.

business applications, screening potential employees, or providing information for training needs. Counselors may use the information for focusing their therapy on a person's personality. Personal analyses are used for compatibility and for self-assessments. It is also used in legal situations. The handwriting expert uses at least 300 different handwriting features to interpret the particular blend of handwriting features. By examining a sample of a person's handwriting, a handwriting expert can identify the way certain features of the letters interact. (No single handwriting sample will include all 300 different features.) Among the features a handwriting expert must analyze are slant, pressure, size, upper and lower case, line and word spacing, angle, and margins.

Pitfalls

Depending on the job, competition may be very tight.

Perks

Document analysis, especially in the forensic field, is a fascinating career that always involves something different.

Get a Jump on the Job

Read everything you can find about document analysis. Take an interdisciplinary approach to academics, leaning toward the liberal arts.

Linda James, forensic document examiner

As her youngest daughter finished high school, Linda James started to think about going back to college and finishing her degree in speech pathology—but she realized she was losing interest. "One night I was watching a black-and-white rerun of *Perry Mason*, and there was a handwriting expert, testifying," James recalls. "I wondered what it would take to become a handwriting expert."

After checking it out, she realized there was no school that offered a degree, but that it did require specialized training. She enrolled in a school with a state-approved curriculum. "After 18 exams and three years of apprenticeship," she says, "I was ready to begin a full-time career as a document and handwriting examiner."

Next, she took an additional course to earn a certificate in forensic science, and then went on to reenroll in college for a degree in criminal justice. "A short time later, a forensic document examination course became available, and after taking the course I was asked to be the instructor." She taught this course for about five years. She is now licensed by the state of Texas to teach law enforcement officers what she does.

In 1995, she met all the requirements of the National Association of Document Examiners (NADE) for certification. (NADE is a certifying body for those wanting to be board certified in document examination.) To become certified, she had to take a written exam at the yearly educational conference and then take an oral exam before a jury and judge (a mock trial by her peers) and the certifying committee of NADE. If you pass this oral exam, you're considered

(continues)

(continued)

board certified and can use the title of CDE (certified document examiner) after your name. The title of "diplomate" requires that you be board certified for 10 years and submit certain information concerning your cases and supply all documentation. Recently, she attended and completed a 45-hour forensic course on the latest document examination equipment at the College Notre-Dame-de-Foy, Canada.

James has owned her own company for almost 15 years. She loves working on the cases, but she isn't so thrilled with the paperwork and responsibility required in running her own company. "At the same time," she confesses, "I like the freedom of setting my own hours."

She's worked on all kinds of cases all around the world—and also helped with cases involving September 11 envelopes and President Bush/National Guard documents.

James advises anyone interested in this field to first get a degree in either forensic science or criminal justice, and then enroll in a course that specializes in document examination. "Be sure the curriculum has been approved by a state agency," she warns. "There are people who are claiming they are a university that can certify you to be a document examiner, so be sure to check out where they got that declaration." After completing all your education, you can then apprentice to a credible document examiner.

"I love my work," she says. "When testifying at depositions and/or trials the document examiner is there to present the truth." Using certain scientific equipment, she can discover hidden facts and details the perpetrator doesn't even know exist. "I've handled cases and traveled all over the world, testifying in Singapore and Alaska. It's adventurous, which I love."

DOLPHIN RESEARCHER

OVERVIEW

If you were captivated by old footage of the TV show *Flipper*, you aren't alone—just about everybody loves these creatures. In fact, so many people are fascinated by these friendly mammals that there are more researchers than research jobs in this field.

There are lots of ways to work with dolphins, depending on what your interests are. Some researchers major in biology and study the dolphins' physical processes. Some biologists take a more global view, studying the characteristics of an entire population, such as the dolphins' home range, diet, or social groupings. Most biologists typically study wild populations of dolphins.

When studying wild populations, marine biologists usually travel far from home, out into the oceans to directly observe dolphins in their natural environment. Because behavioral research with wild dolphins is illegal under the Marine Mammal Protection Act (since it involves changing their behavior), you can't study behavior in wild populations. Instead, researchers record their sounds, photograph them to try to track different individuals, and keep detailed records of their behavior. Other researchers might use binoculars to study dolphins from land, keeping track of the number of animals or how they interact with boaters or swimmers.

AT A GLANCE

Salary Range

Average salary is about $40,000 a year. Salaries vary a great deal among marine mammal scientists, depending on where you work. Government and industry pay the most. Salary levels rise with experience and graduate degrees, but are still fairly low considering the amount of experience and education required.

Education/Experience

Most entry-level jobs in marine mammal science require a bachelor of science degree with a major in biology, chemistry, physics, geology, or psychology. A minor in any science, mathematics, or engineering is helpful. Good language and technical writing skills are essential. You may be surprised to find that you may not get a chance to take a marine mammal class until graduate school. When choosing a grad school to attend, you should first be accepted by a graduate advisor at that university who shares your research interests. Dual majors or interdisciplinary training will broaden your research and career opportunities. As an alternative, you could become a veterinarian, with the ultimate hope of understanding mammalian anatomy, physiology, and biochemistry and understanding the biology of mammals and their ailments.

Personal Attributes

Patience, interest in marine mammals, curiosity, perseverance.

Requirements

Graduate degree in biology or marine mammal-related science.

Outlook

Tight. There are far more people interested in working with dolphins and conducting dolphin research than there are openings.

Marine researchers who are psychologists are more likely to be interested the way dolphins think critically, analyze, and solve problems. Some animal psychologists study dolphin methods of communication and language. Most psychologists study captured individual dolphins being cared for by humans. It's not easy observing dolphins in the wild, swimming quickly underwater, so many projects undertaken by psychologists are carried out in marine facilities with captive populations. These types of studies usually focus on behavior or communication. As an animal psychologist who specializes in dolphin research, you might spend your time recording details about specific behaviors during social interactions among dolphins. Or you might watch the dolphins' response to new stimuli in the animal's environment, such as a mirror placed at one end of a pool. Will the dolphin notice the mirror and try to interact with it? Other scientists might study development of infant dolphins, mother-calf relationships, or the relationship between whistles and behaviors. Or you might study what the dolphins can hear, how good their eyesight

Kathleen Dudzinski, dolphin researcher

It seems to Dr. Kathleen Dudzinski that she's always loved the ocean. "My family and I went to Cape Cod each summer for vacation," she explains. "I have always loved animals...I actively participated in Vo-Ag [vocational agriculture] and FFA [Future Farmers of America] in high school, worked at a veterinary clinic, and raised chickens in my backyard." But it wasn't until the summer after her sophomore year in college that she realized she could transform her love of animals and the ocean into a career. As an intern with a whale watching company, she worked seven days a week, 12 hours a day. "I loved every minute of it," she explains on her Web site. "After that summer I read all I could about dolphins and whales and wrote to scientists for more information."

She admits that there were many people along the way who tried to dissuade her from studying dolphins because there are so few job openings. "But I knew what I wanted to do and what my passion was," she says. "I strongly believe that a person should find their passion, the thing that truly makes them happy, and then pursue it. Life is too short to be unhappy."

After getting her first marine mammal experience with the Atlantic Cetacean Research Center in 1987, Dudzinski studied how Atlantic spotted dolphins in the Bahamas communicate with each other. She graduated from the University of Connecticut with a B.S. in biological sciences in 1989 and got a doctorate in wildlife and fisheries sciences with a focus on dolphin communication and behavior in 1996. During a National Science Foundation fellowship, she studied the communication and behavior among Atlantic spotted dolphins in Bahamian waters and researched bottlenose dolphins in the Gulf of Mexico, Belize, Japan, and in two dolphin aquariums ("Dolphinaria") in Europe. She has also helped design and build a new system for simultaneously recording the behavior and vocalizations of dolphins underwater.

Dr. Dudzinski is dedicated to studying dolphin-to-dolphin communication in the wild, which

is, and how well they communicate or imitate. Some researchers study the dolphins' ability to understand and create language.

There are other areas of research in which both biologists and psychologists may conduct research, such as in echolocation—the way a dolphin is an active area of research by both biologists and psychologists. A biologist may study what physical structures in the dolphins' body produce echolocation clicks, or the way the clicks sound. A psychologist might study what type of information echolocation produces—is it an image or a pattern of sounds that the dolphins hear?

Finally, vets or researchers with medical backgrounds may study dolphin health, by collecting blood samples or by studying animals that have died from stranding themselves on the beach.

Pitfalls

It can be difficult to land a job in this field—*everyone*, it seems, wants to work with dolphins. Once you do get a job, you won't be earning much money at it. Although research with wild dolphins

takes her to remote parts of the world where she studies dolphins in exciting and sometimes even dangerous locations. Although scientists have been observing dolphins in captivity for nearly a century, underwater research on dolphins in the wild has only taken place for about 20 years. Currently, her research was highlighted in the IMAX movie *Dolphins*, and today she's the director of the Dolphin Communication Project (DCP) in Mystic, Connecticut. She is also focusing her attention on research into dolphin communication in the Bahamas and Japan and on the development of education programs with DCP as she develops a new research program on dolphin behavior and communication in Honduras.

While Dudzinski is dedicated to her study of dolphins in the wild, she is also dedicated to exposing others to their world. Some scientists feel that dolphin watching and swimming with dolphins can cause stress, disrupt the animals' feeding patterns, and even risk separating family systems. It's been illegal to swim with wild dolphins in the United States since passage of the Marine Mammal Protection Act in 1972. Since worldwide interest in dolphins is expanding, however, Dudzinski believes the best thing to do is teach people how to swim with the animals responsibly.

If you're interested in becoming a marine biologist, she suggests that you check out possible internship or volunteer programs. She notes that it's not enough just to want to study dolphins—you have to narrow down your interest and figure out specifically what you'd like to focus on.

"Swimming with dolphins has taught me that I don't need to rely on language to understand the meaning of an exchange between individuals," she explains. Although she loves her work, "life is meant to be enjoyed and shared. I guess you could say that dolphins have taught me to enjoy my playtime."

sounds exciting, the research can be repetitive and monotonous. You'll have to cope with often harsh weather and ocean seas, and you'll have a lot of boring work to do back at the lab, analyzing results.

Perks

Despite the competition for jobs and the low pay, if you love marine science and dolphins and you are interested in research, there can be few jobs more exciting or rewarding than interacting, working with, and learning from another species far different from our own.

Get a Jump on the Job

While you're still in high school, you should study science, biology, math, computer science, and a foreign language (dolphin research occurs all over the world). Try to get a job or volunteer in museums, zoos, aquaria, or with veterinarians. These valuable experiences will help you discover what you like to do and what you're good at, as well as help you make contacts within the field. There are many professional Web sites, books, and career guides you can consult for further information. Remember, if your goal is to be a marine mammal scientist, you must first be a good scientist.

ENTOMOLOGIST

OVERVIEW

Roaches, ants, beetles, termites—it's all in a day's work for an entomologist. If thinking about these buzzing, crawling, creeping critters doesn't drive you buggy, there may be a future for you in bug science. An entomologist is a scientist who studies insect habits, life cycles, classifications, and daily life.

There are two main categories of entomologists: basic and applied. Applied entomologists primarily study insects that have either positive or negative direct interaction with people, while basic entomologists seek to learn about various aspects of insects that don't directly interact with people. Applied entomologists may study how to control an insect that is a nuisance to crops, such as the corn borer or soybean aphid. Or they may seek to find answers to help prevent diseases in honeybees.

Some entomologists work at classifying insects, others work to come up with new ways of controlling them, and still others work with other scientists to develop vaccines against insects that spread disease. Some work in research positions, while others may be employed by large pest control companies. Entomologists may be called upon to determine the types and numbers of insects found in a particular area, or to implement pest management programs. Many entomologists specialize in integrated pest management (IPM), which combines a variety of pest control practices (sanitary, chemical, and biological) under one umbrella. Entomologists also may work with beekeeping operations, large agricultural operations, or

AT A GLANCE

Salary Range

Salaries for entomologists range between $29,260 and $71,270. The average salary for an entomologist is $47,740.

Education/Experience

You'll need at least a bachelor of science degree in entomology. Many jobs require a master's degree or even a doctorate.

Personal Attributes

You should have a keen sense of curiosity and be able to work creatively to solve problems. You should have a real interest and respect for insects, and the patience to work with them for long periods of time. You'll also need to be able to communicate effectively and work in cooperation with your colleagues. Good writing skills are a plus, as are good organizational skills and a good memory.

Requirements

Certain security clearances may be required for entomology jobs in government, pharmaceutical or chemical manufacturing firms, and museums.

Outlook

Job growth for entomologists is expected to be about average through 2012, increasing by between 10 and 20 percent, according to the U.S. Bureau of Labor Statistics.

in jobs that enforce insect controls and regulations.

If you decide to become an entomologist, you might discover new types of insects and spend your days carefully studying them to learn about their habits, background, anatomy, and physiology. You might test pesticides in the lab and in the field to see which chemicals work most effectively on different types of insects in

Dr. Karen Oberhauser, entomologist

Dr. Karen Oberhauser was always fascinated with animal life, but she only started working with insects once she got to graduate school. Eventually, she focused on monarch butterflies. As an adjunct professor of ecology, evolution, and behavior at the University of Minnesota, she's become increasingly active in taking entomology into the schools across her region and beyond.

"For the last five years, I've become more and more involved in sharing my work with people outside of the 'ivory tower' of colleges and universities," Oberhauser explains. "I work with teachers and precollege students in Minnesota and throughout the United States using monarchs to teach about biology, conservation, and the process of science."

Oberhauser spent 11 years studying for this position; she holds an undergraduate biology degree from Harvard, a science education degree from the University of Wisconsin at Madison, and a Ph.D. in ecology, evolution, and behavior from the University of Minnesota. A basic entomologist, she studies the reproductive habits of monarch butterflies. Ironically, Oberhauser says, much of her current research concerns the effect that humans have on butterflies—and she's worried about the decreasing habitat available for monarchs and other butterflies. "When we cut down forests in Mexico where they spend the winter, or build houses or parking lots on habitat that contains milkweed, we decrease the amount of habitat that is available for them," she explains.

She hopes that the hours she spends researching and documenting the habits of the butterflies may impact the way that they are considered and treated. "I hope that the research I do may be used to help us make decisions that will not have such a large impact on the species," Oberhauser says.

While teaching keeps her inside for much of her time, Oberhauser still finds time to spend in the field. "I often spend all day, and sometimes all week, in the field," she says. "I study monarchs in Minnesota, Wisconsin, Texas, and Mexico, and often travel to wherever they are in season."

If you're interested in pursuing entomology as a career, Oberhauser suggests that you get up off that sofa and head outside. You may see the occasional spider or ant inside your house, but the real bug action is outside, just waiting for you to discover and explore. She also recommends that you take a lot of science classes, study hard, and get involved with any sort of research project that might come your way. Any type of research experience, she says, will be valuable.

Oberhauser enjoys her work, particularly the time she spends in the field studying monarch butterflies, but the time spent teaching and advocating for monarchs is a nice balance to the fieldwork, she says. "I love the diversity of activities that I'm involved with," Oberhauser explains. "I love learning more about monarchs every year. And I also love sharing what I learn with other people, and feeling that I may be making a difference in making the world a better place for monarchs, other organisms, and people."

different conditions. Or you might work to develop nonchemical insect controls through the use of predators, parasites, or genetics.

You may study the effects that insects have on forests, human and animal health, and agriculture, run public awareness programs concerning insects, or work to figure out how to keep potentially harmful insects from being transported from one part of the world to another. Entomologists also organize insect exhibits for museums.

You'll find entomologists in a wide variety of organizations and companies, working for the government, pharmaceutical and chemical producers, museums, educational facilities, and large pest control companies. Some serve as consultants to businesses, industry, and individuals, while others teach in high schools, colleges, and universities.

As an entomologist, the career path you choose depends on your particular interests and your level of education. Job competition for top-level entomology jobs is extremely keen, however, meaning that some Ph.D.s are willing to take jobs for which those with lesser degrees may qualify.

Pitfalls

Entomologists study insects in laboratories and in the field, so there will be times that you'll need to be out in the elements, sometimes in remote locations for long periods of time. You also may risk exposure to chemicals used in the control of pests, or to dangerous pests themselves.

Perks

The study of insects can be exciting, and it's vitally important work. Insects are an important part of the chain of life, so they must be nurtured and protected, but they also must be controlled in order to coexist with animals and humans. There are many job opportunities available for entomologists, and it's fairly easy to move around from one job specialty to another.

Get a Jump on the Job

If you haven't ever put together an insect collection, now might be the time to start one. Be sure to research each addition carefully, working to keep good, organized notes and making sure you record all pertinent information. There are a lot of good books out there that can teach you a lot about insects and entomology (see the Read More About It section at the back of this book for some suggestions), and the Internet is full of news and information concerning insects. Check out some undergraduate entomology program requirements and see if you can get a jump on some of the classes you'll need once you get to college. If your school offers advanced biology or physiology courses, for instance, look into taking them.

FINGERPRINT ANALYST

OVERVIEW

Chances are that your knowledge of fingerprint analysis comes mostly from TV crime shows. If that's the case, you're going to have to reshape how you think about the job. According to those who actually work as fingerprint analysts, the TV version is nothing like the real thing!

It might look dashing, exciting, and glamorous on TV, but in reality fingerprint analysis can be tedious, demanding work, requiring long hours of concentration. Although you seldom see the TV crime scene people looking dirty, exhausted, and harried, that's often the case for real fingerprint analysts.

While most people think of a fingerprint analyst as the guy dusting furniture and glassware at a crime scene, in fact you'll find these analysts doing a variety of tasks. It's the fingerprint analyst who fingerprints those who've been arrested to determine if they are who they say they are. This also allows law enforcement personnel to find out if a criminal is wanted elsewhere for other crimes or if he or she has had trouble with the law in the past. Fingerprint analysts must also sometimes record the fingerprints of corpses and may be called to testify in court cases concerning a wrongful death or other crime. Analysts also fingerprint people applying for jobs that require background checks. Some communities run programs to fingerprint kids so they can be identified if they're ever lost or kidnapped.

AT A GLANCE

Salary Range
An experienced fingerprint analyst can expect to earn about $40,000 a year, but salaries vary depending on location and type of employer. The FBI, for example, pays a fingerprint analyst much more than a small-town police department.

Education/Experience
You'll need at least a high school education or an equivalency degree; some agencies require an associate of arts degree or some postsecondary training in police science or criminology. Some vocational schools and community colleges offer excellent programs in law enforcement or emergency services. Some agencies will only accept candidates with prior experience.

Personal Attributes
You need to be patient, attentive to detail, and exacting. You'll need to be willing to spend long periods of time to determine one key fact in a case. You should have a grasp on technological methods, and you should be in reasonable physical condition.

Requirements
Federal, state, county, and local agencies may require a civil service exam. You may need certification of vision and mental capacity. You'll probably need to have a valid driver's license and be able to use a computer. Most agencies will require drug tests and a background check to make sure you have no history of criminal activity. Some government jobs require that you be of a certain age—typically between 21 and 37—when starting a job.

Outlook
Fingerprint analyst jobs are expected to increase at a greater than average rate by 2012, according to government predictions, in part because of heightened security concerns. However, many of these jobs will be lower-paying positions, or in urban areas with high crime rates. The highest-paying jobs will remain very competitive.

Still, the best-known tasks of a fingerprint analyst lie in the field, when latent fingerprint analysts arrive at a crime scene to uncover fingerprints—either visible or invisible (latent). This involves dusting for prints, a dirty job, according to those who've done it. Any prints that turn up can then be run through the automated files that contain the fingerprints of any known suspects or held until a suspect is found.

To make a match (or a "positive identification"), fingerprint analysts are taught to compare an individual's print with files of other fingerprints of known criminals. In the old days, this was all done by hand. Analysts would search thousands and thousands of fingerprints cards, hoping to find a match. Today computers compare prints using automated files from which analysts can access a subject's personal information such as age, sex, and address, as well as fingerprint images.

Fingerprint analysts may work in situations ranging from local police departments to the FBI. Many city and county police forces hire fingerprint analysts, although in some departments, police

Gary W. Jones, fingerprint analyst

Gary Jones has been a fingerprint analyst for more than 40 years, most of which were spent working for the FBI. He figures that he's seen just about everything there is to see when it comes to crime.

"I worked cases involving every sort of crime, from simple burglaries to multiple homicides," says Jones, of Summerfield, Florida. He began his career with the FBI after completing four years of military service. Early on, he was responsible for classifying and searching fingerprint cards, which, in those days, were handled manually. Classifying fingerprints is the complex and technical process of examining a print for particular pattern, position, and size. Learning how to do this properly requires extensive training, Jones says. "It takes at least 40 hours of classroom instruction to learn just the basics of fingerprint classification."

Once the prints had been classified, Jones would search particular files to see if he could find a match. Through that process, he could determine if there had been a prior arrest, or if the subject was using a false name.

Jones worked as a fingerprint classifier for six years, during which time he compared about 7 million fingerprints. He then moved up to the FBI's latent fingerprint section and spent a year training on the specifics of latent print work. After 27 years in the latent section, he retired from the FBI as a supervisory fingerprint specialist in 1997 and now runs his own fingerprint analysis business.

While office jobs are more predictable, Jones says there was no typical day for him when he was working in the field. Every day was different. "TV programs such as CSI give a very unrealistic view of the world of forensics," Jones says. "The examiners are always young and hip, with the women wearing $500 outfits and high heels that never get dirty. The truth is that

(continues)

(continued)

forensics is just plain, hard work, and a person will find that out when they spend a day dusting with black fingerprint powder. At the end of the day, you are filthy, exhausted, looking like a coal miner."

However, if you're truly interested in being a fingerprint analyst, you may find it to be a rewarding career. "I love it and would never consider doing anything else," Jones says.

There's also great satisfaction in knowing that you helped to identify the guilty and eliminate the innocent. "To me, the most enjoyable aspect of being a fingerprint examiner is the satisfaction of aiding in the solving of a crime or else exonerating innocent individuals," Jones says. "Remember, if 10 suspects are named as possibly being involved in a particular crime, and I identify one of those as being the person who committed the crime, I have also exonerated nine other people."

If you want to be a fingerprint analyst, you should take as many science courses as possible. You could begin by applying to a law enforcement agency as a crime scene technician, and then working your way into fingerprint work from there. Be sure to let your supervisor know you're interested in fingerprint analysis, Jones notes. But there's more than one path to becoming a fingerprint analyst. "It's like being a race car driver," he says. "There is no standard path, and it's an experience-driven profession. There is no college that you can go to and graduate as a fingerprint expert."

Jones also advises that individuals who want to enter the field of fingerprint analysis should be self-motivated and meticulous about their work. "It is a field that demands those qualities," Jones says.

officers or clerical workers perform fingerprint duties. Some self-employed fingerprint analysts offer their services to private attorneys, individuals, and police departments without an analyst on staff.

Pitfalls

Analyzing fingerprints can be extremely tedious, calling for long periods of intense concentration. It also can be very stressful because you're always under pressure to solve a crime. The job involves long, late hours working different shifts and sometimes seeing disturbing sights.

Perks

Fingerprint work is varied and interesting, and you'll usually form close bonds with your coworkers. If crime and law enforcement attracts you, this is one specialty that can really hold your interest.

Get a Jump on the Job

Science courses are important—particularly chemistry. Practice being detail oriented in your tasks and observant. Read books about analyzing fingerprints.

FIRE SCIENTIST

OVERVIEW

If you can take the heat, the market for fire science majors is booming. Specializing in experiments involving flame, fire scientists study fire and its role in nature, especially how it affects forest ecology. From the tropical forest of Puerto Rico to the expanses of rangelands in the west, fire scientists conduct research and scientific analysis to better understand how fire can hurt or help the outdoors. They work as consultants and foresters, evaluating and monitoring forest or grassland ecosystems for their interactions with fire.

Wildfires can be enormous, stretching over several states, and unpredictable, claiming the lives of many firefighters every year. But fire scientists understand that wildfires are natural and inevitable, and play an important role in many ecosystems. Unfortunately, the encroachment of human development into forests and grasslands means that fire and people often come uncomfortably close.

In addition, fire scientists are no strangers to controversy. The fire management policy of most of the past century has been to suppress and prevent forest fires. However upsetting these fires were, what these policies overlooked was the extreme importance of fires to many ecosystems, particularly in the western United States, which cannot function without a natural cycle of fire. Fire scientists believe that fires are inevitable and that suppression practices have allowed a heavy build-up of dead vegetation and plants. As a result,

when fires do occur, they burn hotter and faster, are harder to control, and cause devastating economic and ecological damage.

Instead, fire scientists recommend prescribed burns as a way to simulate the natural fire ecology of wildlands, along with thinning dead vegetation and dense undergrowth and tree stands, removing non-native species. As a result, many agencies use prescribed burns as part of their natural resource management. For a

Wallace Covington, Ph.D., fire scientist and forest ecologist

Wally Covington is passionate about forests. A national leader in forest restoration research, he earned a Ph.D. in ecosystem sciences from Yale University in 1976. He founded and directs the Ecological Restoration Institute (ERI) at Northern Arizona University (NAU), which works on healing fire-adapted ecosystems in western North America. The ERI works with the public, land management agencies, nongovernmental organizations, and researchers to heal ailing forests while reducing threats of unnatural wildfire.

Dr. Covington has received national and international recognition for his work in forest ecosystem health, restoration ecology, and fire effects on forest ecosystems. He was recognized as an Outstanding Teaching Scholar by NAU in 1990 for his dedication to involving undergraduates in his research projects and bringing research results into the classroom. He's worked with students as a professor of forest ecology at the university since 1975.

"Throughout my career, I've applied my academic skills to real world problems," he explains, "teaching research methods, forest ecology and restoration, and forest, range, wildlife, watershed, recreation, and wildland management.

"I've been working in long-term research on fire ecology and management in ponderosa pine and related ecosystems since I moved to Northern Arizona University in 1975." In addition to his publications on forest restoration, he has co-authored scientific papers on fire effects, prescribed burning, thinning, operations research, silviculture, range management, wildlife effects, multiresource management, forest health, and natural resource conservation.

Humans have damaged or destroyed most ecosystems in the world. Ecological restoration seeks to heal that damage by reestablishing native species of plants and trees. Dr. Covington and his colleagues try to understand and reverse the causes of ecological damage by reintroducing natural fire regimes, removing invasive species, thinning overly dense forest stands, and seeding native plants.

prescribed burn, fire scientists evaluate the ecosystem, determine safety needs, and light a fire under controlled conditions. This fire usually burns out the undergrowth of a forest or grassland, allowing new plants to sprout after the fire.

Other tools fire scientists use include manual or mechanical removal of brush. In environmentally-sensitive areas, some fire scientists have recommended using goats to clear understory plants and grasses.

But there's more to the work of a fire scientist than prescribed burns. These scientists specifically study natural fire regimes for different ecosystem types, the effects of different kinds of fire on the landscape, the behavior of fire under different conditions, the effectiveness of foams and retardants and the effects of different tactics used to put fires out. Fire science also addresses restoration and rehabilitation of wildlands after fire moves across watersheds, bringing new insights into enhancing native species of trees and plants.

Pitfalls

Fire science can be controversial, pitting scientists against environmentalists,

Over the past 150 years, most forests in the southwestern United States have been damaged because of logging, grazing, fire suppression, and invasive non-native plant species. As a result, many areas—especially in ponderosa pine forests—have been taken over by dense thickets of young trees that are very susceptible to fire. Dr. Covington and his colleagues are trying to restore these forests by starting low-intensity surface fires more often—the type of natural event that formerly maintained forests.

"Nowhere is the rate of loss as great as it is in landscapes once dominated by open long-needled pine savannas and forests," according to Dr. Covington. "These endangered ecosystems threaten all species, including humans that depend upon them for habitat."

His research has focused on western long-needled pine ecosystems—especially the ponderosa pine. He's trying to find out the kind of conditions that existed when the ponderosa pine lived before the Europeans came, and what recent changes in the pine's conditions occurred. He designs experimental research projects to restore natural conditions in specific areas to compare them to other land management treatments and to determine practical ways to restore the ecological system. In addition to small-plot studies, Covington and his colleagues are now working cooperatively with federal agencies on ecosystem management experiments ranging in size from 50 to 600 acres. "Working with partners, the [ERI] has built strong support for restoration-based fuel treatments," he says. "Ecological restoration deals with research and management experimentation to determine ways for safely restoring degraded ecological systems to nearly natural conditions," he says. The goal of this process, he says, is to restore ecosystem health problems by sticking to the natural patterns of the forest as much as possible.

although both insist they are trying to save the nation's forests.

Perks

If you love the outdoors and nature, working to protect the natural resources of the United States can be a wonderful way to make a living.

Get a Jump on the Job

Read everything you can about forest ecology and try volunteering at your local parks or forests, or your local fire department, to learn more about fire and what it can do. Take lots of biology and chemistry classes in high school, along with ecology if your school offers it.

FLIGHT NURSE

OVERVIEW

If you've ever seen a helicopter land at the scene of an accident—in real life or on TV—you've probably noticed the medical personnel jumping out to assist the patient. These can be exciting jobs for the right person: Aeromedical vehicles are like flying ambulances, and experienced medical personnel are needed to staff them. Flight nurses are experienced, highly trained registered nurses who help to rescue and transport seriously ill or injured patients. Aeromedical helicopters and planes fly to the scenes of accidents and also fly from hospital to hospital to transport patients from one facility to another. The Air Force also trains and utilizes flight nurses, either as reservists or active duty personnel.

On a typical workday, the flight nurse starts by checking all the equipment that might be needed for a flight and makes sure that the helicopter is fully stocked and ready to go. The team members meet at the beginning of each shift to review weather conditions, determine whether all the aircraft are flying, and discuss any safety issues. After the meeting, the flight nurse might check up on patients who have recently been treated. The flight nurse is also always prepared to fly.

Air medical transport services are run both by hospital systems and private providers. Flight nurses are usually assigned to a 12- or 24-hour shift at either a hospital medical flight program or a satellite base outside a hospital. (Although some aeromedical flights are scheduled, most fly on an emergency basis.)

AT A GLANCE

Salary Range

The average pay for all registered nurses is $48,090, with a range of between $33,970 and $69,670. Flight nurses must be highly experienced, so their salaries tend to be at the upper end of the range.

Education/Experience

You'll need to be a registered nurse, which requires that you go to a hospital nursing program or a college that offers a registered nursing program. Some states also require that you have a bachelor of science in nursing degree in addition to nursing certification.

Personal Attributes

You should be caring and compassionate but able to remain calm and composed when under pressure. You must be tolerant of air travel and cramped conditions and able to respond quickly to emergencies and make quick decisions.

Requirements

Many flight nurse programs require that you've had at least a couple of years experience in critical care or emergency care, but every flight program has its own experience requirements. Some programs also require that you be certified as an emergency medical technician or have other training and certification, such as Advanced Cardiac Life Support, Pediatric Advanced Life Support, or Neonatal Resuscitation. If you want to be a military flight nurse, you need to be a member of the Air Force, less than 47 years old, meet the criteria for a Class III flight physical, complete basic training, complete the six-week Air Force flight nurse training program, and meet the Air Force officer commissioning criteria.

Outlook

While the job situation for all registered nurses is expected to improve faster than average—between 21 and 35 percent by 2012—flight nursing is a competitive field, so job growth will be slower. Still, the number of flight nurses will continue to increase as more medical flight programs are put into place.

Helicopters and planes are used for air medical transport. Helicopters may accommodate one or two patients, the pilot, and the medical staff, which may include two flight nurses or a flight nurse and a respiratory therapist. A medical plane may be needed if you're going to be traveling a long distance, the patient must be moved faster than a helicopter can fly, or if weather isn't safe for a helicopter.

As a flight nurse, you've got to be comfortable treating patients with just about any kind of injury or illness. You might find yourself inserting a chest or breathing tube, transfusing blood, or even using a needle to remove fluid from the sac surrounding the heart. It's all in a day's work for a flight nurse, who may make three or four flights a day.

In addition to regular flight duties, these specialist nurses typically juggle other duties as well, such as speaking to the community about aeromedical transport, training local emergency medical service personnel, or teaching classes on topics concerning emergency medical services.

Pitfalls

Treating a seriously injured patient while you're flying in a helicopter is no easy task

Marcie Johnson, flight nurse

Marcie Johnson can imagine nothing better than being paid to work as a nurse on a plane or helicopter. "Getting paid to be a nurse and fly is just too good to be true for me," Johnson says. "I wanted to be a flight nurse because I love flying so much. I really love being in the air."

Johnson works for Vanderbilt LifeFlight, an air medical program based at Vanderbilt Hospital in Nashville, Tennessee. The program operates out of four satellite stations, aimed at making air transport available to people in a wider geographical area. She works as a team with a second flight nurse, a pilot, and a flight communications person.

"We are a tight-knit team at LifeFlight," Johnson says. "As you can well imagine, this can sometimes be a stressful job. When you share experiences that are intense, you form a bond similar to that of a family."

Just like EMS paramedics, flight nurses never know when they'll have a flight until they're dispatched. They're always on call. And although caring for patients is the primary goal of a flight nurse, Johnson says that even patient care is second to the safety of the operating aircraft. "Safety is our number one product, because we are no benefit to the public unless we operate safely," Johnson says. "Our second product is excellent patient care."

While Johnson loves her work, she warns that the job requires a lot of training—you'll need to be willing to work hard. "You must have a minimum of three years of nursing experience, preferably in the intensive care unit or the emergency department," Johnson says. "It's good to get experience with both adults and pediatrics, because that's what you'll need to know when you're flying. The helicopters are used for acute patients of all kinds—trauma, medical, cardiac, burns, you name it. A flight nurse should be very well rounded and have a vast experience base."

Yet while the work is difficult, it also is extremely rewarding. "I really like the patient contact and being able to make a difference for someone in a critical point in their life," Johnson says. "That is the reward for me."

and can be extremely stressful. Along the way, you're bound to see some disturbing (even horrific) sights as you respond to highway accidents, crime scenes, abuse cases, fires, or drownings. Because flight nursing is a competitive field, you may need to work in other areas of nursing while you look for a job.

Perks

Aeromedical crews generally are committed to their work and work together well as a team. This makes for a rewarding work experience. Most nurses also find it rewarding to be able to help patients, especially those who are seriously injured or sick.

Get a Jump on the Job

Some aeromedical services will permit passengers to ride along on a flight if they're at least 18 years old and enrolled as a student in a medical field. You'd need to contact emergency services in your area to see if they offer that opportunity. If you're interested in being a military flight nurse, you could contact an Air Force recruiter to get more information about qualifications and requirements. In the meantime, learn everything that you can about being a flight nurse, take lots of science courses in preparation for a nursing career, and start looking into colleges and schools that offer good nursing programs.

FORENSIC SCULPTOR

OVERVIEW

Armed with just a skull, maybe a strand of hair, some artifacts, and a pile of clay, forensic sculptors can recreate a face and even a personality, helping the police solve crimes and identify victims. Forensic facial reconstruction, after all, is more science than art. It's a skill of particular value when police find a skeleton but have no idea who the person was. Skeletons leave no fingerprints and dental records can only reveal a person's name when X rays or special dental work have been done to provide comparison. Therefore, in the case of an unidentified skeleton, police call on a forensic reconstruction sculptor to create a recognizable cast of the person's face and expression.

In the 1800s, a German anatomist and a sculptor decided to try to reproduce the likeness of prehistoric people. Using many cadavers, they came up with a standardized system of facial tissue thickness charts. Criminologists stumbled onto this work in the mid-20th century and have been using it ever since to sculpt faces over skulls.

Facial sculpting differs from composite drawing in that you don't have a witness to give you an idea of what the person looked like. With facial reconstruction, the artist guesses what the person looked like, while trying to be as accurate as possible so that something about the sculpture attracts the attention of a family member or friend.

In general, forensic sculptors take advantage of the fact that there are certain racial characteristics common among

humans. The architecture of facial bones gives each face the unique characteristics that in most cases can spark recognition in a viewer. For example, a person of Asian descent will typically have a flat face and rather vertical cranium, as well as pronounced sutures (the wavy lines on the skull). The sutures in younger people also tend to be more pronounced. A person of African descent tends to have a protruding mouth and sloping cranium, while those of

European descent have a cranium some-what in the middle (neither drastically sloping nor vertical). Men tend to have more prominent ridges on the forehead, while the foreheads of women tend to be more rounded. All these data about differ-ent races, genders, and ages are kept in a handbook the artists use when establishing tissue markers and laying clay.

Using precise anthropological data, standard tissue depths are calculated from measurements at 21 specific locations across the face. Combining these scientific data and artistic skills, narrow strips of clay are then applied to the skull to con-nect the tissue depth markers on the face and across the cranium; the grid sections that are formed by the strips will be filled

Ann Morland, forensic facial reconstruction specialist

In the late 1960s, Ann Morland saw a news report about two people reconstructing a face from a skull that was later identified when the face was recognized. "It caught my attention," she says, "and I knew that was what I wanted to do. From that moment, I started looking for the data and techniques they were using, guided by the memory of those two people and the work they did."

Eventually, she was able to track down some information about the process, and she was able to buy a skull replica from a ceramic store to try her own first facial reconstruction. "I continued my search for new information and each time I found some data, I would do another reconstruction," she says. "Over the years, as I found more information, I continued to reconstruct faces over any skull replica I could find," she says. "It wasn't until the 1990s that I found out that the two people I had read about 20 years earlier were Dr. Clyde Snow and Betty Pat Gatliff." (Gatliff is credited with the development of the American method of facial reconstruction.) Eventually, Morland was able to take classes from Betty Pat.

"I learned the techniques that enabled me to finally correct my mistakes," she says. "It gave me a chance to acquire the data that I had had such a hard time finding for so many years. It gave me a new sense of respect for the people who do this work and a great desire to continue on."

Morland considers herself to be a forensic facial reconstruction specialist, of which forensic sculpting is only a part of her job. A forensic facial reconstruction specialist works in four areas: *forensic sculpting*, in which a face is reconstructed on a skull by clay or by drawing; *age progression and fugitive updates*, in which a future face is reconstructed from photographs of the person at an earlier age; *postmortem drawings*, in which a face is reconstructed from a face of a deceased person; and *composite drawing*, in which a face is reconstructed from a victim or witness account.

Those who only reconstruct faces from skulls using clay are called forensic sculptors. Those who only draw composites from a victim's memory are called forensic artists. Those who work in all the four areas are considered forensic facial reconstruction specialists.

When it comes to teaching the American method of facial reconstruction, experts are few and far between. "I'm only one of two people in the world who teach 2-D facial reconstruction by drawing and postmortem drawings," Morland says. (Betty Pat is the other.) "I'm among a

to the proper depth with clay. The cheeks are filled with clay to the depth indicated by markers.

The sculptor makes various measurements to determine nose thickness and length, mouth width, and eye placement. To begin building the nose, a block of clay is cut and placed at the base of the nasal opening; this block indicates the projec-tion and tilt of the nose. Balls of clay representing the nostrils are placed on each side of the nasal opening at a measurement appropriate to the person's race. The remaining portion of the nasal opening is then filled in.

The mouth also begins with a block of clay cut to specific depth, width, and height measurements. The width of the

handful of people who teach composite drawing." Although Morland estimates that there are at least 2,000 trained composite artists and only 20 full-time jobs, there is need for more people in this field. "Our largest obstacle to overcome is educating law enforcement agencies that our expertise is as essential to their work as fingerprints," she says. "Fingerprints have a 10 percent success rate, but the least accomplished composite artist has a 30 to 70 percent success rate." For Morland, her job is endlessly interesting. "There is such a large amount of variety in the things I do," she says. She teaches classes four times a year in forensic facial reconstruction, composites, age progression, and postmortem drawings. She draws composites when needed, and draws postmortem and age progression drawings for clients. "It is always difficult to work cases that involve children, for they are usually missing or deceased," she says, "but they also need a way to go home and our job provides such a way, through forensic sculpting and age progression drawing."

The University of Tennessee offers the only degree in forensic art, through their anthropology department. Betty Pat Gatliff offers classes twice a year in Scottsdale, Arizona, and in Norman, Oklahoma. By 2007, a master's degree in forensic facial reconstruction will be offered through the anthropology department at the University of Alabama at Birmingham.

Police departments hire forensic facial reconstruct specialists to draw composites when there is a surviving victim or witness. Facial sculpting is generally from medical examiners or district attorneys who are trying a case, she explains. Postmortem drawings are requested when there is an unidentified body. "In my case, I have drawn composites for police departments, and drawn postmortems for the DOE Network, a volunteer organization that provides pro bono work for police organizations around the world. My largest client base comes from the unlikely source of trial lawyers. It is cases that involve deceased children that I find the most challenging, and the ones I feel good about having been involved with."

Morland cautions that it's hard to make a living as a forensic sculptor. "Those who do this work can earn a living, but they must offer all the other areas of expertise in this field," she says. Still, she says, "I have come to love this work with great passion, and wonder how I ever lived without it. My goal is to provide opportunities for the younger generation to step into a field of work that is respected for the contributions it makes to society."

mouth is determined by the first six teeth. The block is placed over the teeth and clay is filled in around the mouth to the correct tissue depth. Stains on teeth that remain tell artists where the gums stopped.

To create the eyes, mannequin or prosthetic eyes are set in the orbits of the skull, clay is filled around, and the upper and lower eyelids are applied. Since there can be no way to tell what the eye color should be, brown (the dominate eye color) is always used.

The sculpture is finished by smoothing and molding the clay to create a lifelike appearance, creating the appropriate age patterns (such as wrinkles around the eyes), along with hair, ears, and neck.

The resulting sculpture is only used to spark someone's recognition and suggest a name to investigators. It's not legally possible to positively identify someone based on a facial reconstruction; that requires standard methods of positive identification, such as dental records, X rays, or DNA.

In addition to legal cases, forensic sculptors also work with museums to create visual representations of ancient individuals to help visitors envision the past.

Pitfalls

The work can be gory, and some people might find working with the deceased to be depressing.

Perks

It can be uplifting to suddenly help the police solve a crime or bring closure to a family by providing identification for a loved one who has died without identification.

Get a Jump on the Job

Volunteering with your local police department can open doors. In addition, study those areas that will help you the most in this work: science classes in biology, anatomy, and osteology, and art classes in drawing, sculpting, and pastels or colored pencil.

GEMOLOGIST

OVERVIEW

A jeweler can sell or create jewelry, but a gemologist is trained to be able to identify gemstones and to assess their quality and value. Gemologists work in jewelry stores and department stores; for wholesalers, importers, jewelry designers, auction houses, and gem laboratories; as independent appraisers; in their own businesses; and in other facets of the industry.

They may appraise jewelry for insurance purposes or to determine a selling or starting price at an auction. Some gemologists buy and sell loose stones, while others work with gems that have been made into items of jewelry. Still other gemologists combine jewelry design with their knowledge of gemstones to create fine jewelry for private customers or jewelry stores.

Anyone can take a few classes and then use the "gemologist" label, but it takes lots of training and experience to be able to properly analyze and assess the quality of diamonds and colored gemstones. Gemologists also work with diamonds and gemstones to bring out their best qualities or to place them in jewelry settings. Some gemologists specialize in one stone, such as diamonds or pearls, while others are generalists.

Gemologists must be trained to use specialized and sophisticated equipment, such as spectrometers, which are used in grading diamonds. To grade a diamond, the gemologist must carefully observe the stone, analyzing it under a microscope to determine its cut, color, symmetry, size,

AT A GLANCE

Salary Range

A certified gemologist earns between $22,000 and $70,000 a year, depending on location, experience, expertise, and services offered.

Education/Experience

There are no established educational requirements for a gemologist, but applicable courses are available in trade schools, vocational and technical schools, and through distance-learning centers. Some gemologists learn on the job as apprentices. Art schools and some colleges offer bachelor's and master's degrees in jewelry design, which could speed your way into the industry.

Personal Attributes

You should be good with your hands and have good hand-eye coordination. Patience is a valuable attribute for a gemologist, as is the ability to work with customers and the public. You should have a neat appearance and be able to effectively relate information about gems and their handling.

Requirements

Although gemologists don't need to be certified, you'll have more credibility if you are. There are various institutions that test and certify gemologists, including the prestigious Gemological Institute of America (GIA). Certification can be pursued at the GIA's campus in Carlsbad, California, or through online courses.

Outlook

The demand for gemologists and jewelers is expected to increase as jewelry sales continue to grow. A major share of jewelry purchases are made by people who are 45 or older, a population that is rapidly growing. Replacements will be necessary for master gemologists and jewelers who take years of experience with them when they retire.

Darrell Powell, gemologist

Darrell Powell is a graduate gemologist with certification from the Gemological Institute of America in Carlsbad, California, who runs an extensive jewelry operation in conjunction with a pawn shop in Rockledge, Florida. His extensive training enables him to identify various gemstones and assess their value. This is an important part of his business, in which people often bring in stones and jewelry to sell or to pawn. The training has also instilled in him a real appreciation of gemstones.

"I get to see some really cool and interesting things that the average person doesn't," Powell says. "I've seen some really interesting inclusions, like a garnet inside of a diamond. I've also seen some really high-quality stones that most people don't get to see in the average jewelry store."

Powell's typical day is spent evaluating and appraising gemstones, dealing with customers, and keeping detailed records of every transaction, as required by law. He also cleans and reconditions gemstones, resets jewelry, and gives advice to clients about gemstones.

While diamonds may be the most high-profile gemstone, Powell says they're the least challenging to work with. "Diamonds are about the easiest stones to identify and to grade and do mounted repairs," he says. "You have to remove many other types of stones from their settings so as not to damage them, but diamonds can remain in the setting."

The most challenging stone to work with, Powell says, is the emerald. "Emeralds are very soft," he explains. "They can't take heat during repair. The ultrasound cleaner can break them, and they have a very low durability," he says.

Of all the gemstones he works with, Powell says that opals are his favorites. "The opal is the only gemstone that has that play of color—the many different colors you see when you look at it from all the angles. It has tiny bumps all over it—like a golf ball—so the light refracts in many different ways, producing all those colors. It's the only stone that does that. It's like a rainbow."

Powell became interested in gemology through a family connection, and he finds it fascinating and rewarding. One of his daughters has also started studying with the Gemological Institute of America and is working toward certification as a graduate gemologist. Powell advises anyone interested in the career to try to work with a jeweler who understands gemstones. You'll need to get this kind of experience before you can become established as a respected jeweler or gemologist.

"The jewelry business is a rather closed field," Powell says. "If you're interested, you should try to get some experience in a jewelry store that has qualified people who you can learn from. Then it would be helpful to work as an apprentice and learn the basics."

Powell recommends waiting to take classes from the GIA or another recognized institution until after you've acquired some experience by working in the field. He also recommends trying to find a qualified certified jeweler to serve as a mentor as you learn still more about gemstones.

"There are different ways to enter the business, but training and experience are both vitally important," he says. "Just graduating from the GIA is not a guarantee of a job, [but] it sure helps to have those credentials. It can pave the way and make it easier for you to get started."

clarity, and other characteristics. Once a grading has been determined, a certificate is issued for the diamond.

Most gemologists consider colored gemstones to be more challenging to work with than diamonds, because there are not specific standards for color, clarity, cut, and carat weight measurements. There also are different classifications of colored gemstones: genuine, synthetic, and imitation, as well as a non-permanent treatment, which is actually a coating applied to a colorless topaz to make it appear as a different stone.

Gemologists must work hard to obtain and keep the trust and confidence of customers. They also must be aware of and alert to less-than-honest dealers and handlers who would like to pass off a stone as being something it isn't.

If you like the idea of working for yourself, you could consider working toward having your own jewelry store or jewelry repair shop. A repair service is often included in a jewelry store business.

Pitfalls

The jewelry and gem business is susceptible to ups and downs in the economy.

Working with gems requires a great deal of concentration and exactness, which can be stressful. In addition, jewelry stores have traditionally been the occasional targets of burglars and robbers.

Perks

If you like working with beautiful objects, gemology may be the perfect field. Most gemologists find pleasure in bringing out the best in beautiful stones. The job is not overly demanding physically, although there is the occasional cramp in the neck from sitting too long in one position.

Get a Jump on the Job

If you're old enough, apply for a job in a jewelry store in your area. Be sure to note on your application that you're interested in the possibility of studying gemology as a career. Take geology courses at school to help you learn about and understand the makeup of various stones. Study gems and read books to help you learn how to identify them and get an idea of their value.

GERIATRIC CARE MANAGER

OVERVIEW

You're getting ready to move halfway across the country with your new job, but who will watch out for your elderly mom or dad, still living at home but starting to have some trouble getting around?

The answer is a geriatric care manager—a multi-disciplined specialist with skills and training in a wide range of tasks and services. A geriatric care manager needs to have some medical background, coupled with social work skills, computer savvy, and the ability to work effectively with people who are dealing with difficult decisions and problems. There is no such thing as a typical day in his or her business because no two clients or situations are the same. As a geriatric care manager, you're a combination of medical and legal advisor, baby-sitter, counselor, and an authority on dozens of issues affecting the elderly.

Geriatric care management is a fairly new field, growing ever more popular as the population ages. A geriatric care manager begins by sitting down with the family to assess the situation of the elderly person. The range of services can vary tremendously, but the process almost always begins with an assessment. The manager will address the goals of both the elderly person and the family members and evaluate whether those goals are feasible and how to reach them. If it's determined that the goals are not attainable, the care

AT A GLANCE

Salary Range

About $30,000 to $35,000 a year to start, but there's the potential to earn much more if you get some experience and then start your own business.

Education/Experience

It varies depending on the employer, but you'll probably need a degree in social work or nursing. A licensed practical nursing degree, coupled with some social work coursework, would provide ideal qualifications.

Personal Attributes

You must be a self-motivated problem solver and able to quickly assess a situation and decide on the best course of action. You need to be diplomatic and compassionate, able to work well with elderly people, and not afraid to deal with tough situations. You must be willing and able to perform a variety of services, from pet care to filing Medicare claims.

Requirements

Certification is not necessary but is highly recommended. There are several agencies that provide certification, including the National Academy of Certified Care Managers.

Outlook

The demand for geriatric care managers is expected to increase dramatically as the population ages and people continue living longer. Demand will be higher in some areas of the country than in others due to concentrations of retired and aging people in various locations.

manager will help the client to establish alternate, more realistic goals. Where will Mom or Dad live? What's the condition of the home where the person is living now? What's their health status—are they eating regularly and sleeping okay?

The manager can give advice on tax issues, living wills, power of attorney, insurance matters, guardianship, Medicare and Medicaid, trusts, and so forth. He or she will need to be able to direct family members to the best nursing care facilities, which means the care manager must have firsthand knowledge, or a trusted source

Patricia Antony, geriatric care manager

Discouraged with the reality of life as a physical therapist, Patty Antony of Orlando turned to Florida's aging population for a job when the large rehabilitation company she worked for closed down. Realizing that Florida has lots of elderly people who have no family members living near by, Antony established her own geriatric care management company to fill the void. "I thought that I'd be really good at helping people get their parents sorted out," Antony says. "That was something I seemed to know how to do."

She's a lifesaver for adult children who live in different states and hire her to arrange services for an elderly parent living in the Orlando area. "In our transient society, people don't always live near their families and family members aren't able to care for them," Antony says. "That's just the way things are."

Her job is to take over the caregiver's responsibilities and find the best help available for the elderly parent, providing peace of mind for the children. Antony's company is now in its seventh year. She's moved out of her home into an office and hired several employees to help her handle a client list of about 50 active accounts and 150 more that require occasional or periodical attention.

"I was told that I'd never make a living out of it, but that's certainly turned out not to be true," she says. Although she thoroughly enjoys her work, she admits it's a constant challenge to find solutions to the problems that her clients confront, as she works with attorneys, police officers, hospital personnel, ministers, bankers, social workers, nursing home administrators, counselors, insurance companies, and government agencies.

"There's no standard answer," she says. "We have to work with each client individually. It's never the same. There are no two days alike. It's all over the map." Antony has worked as a dog sitter for a client who fell and broke a hip and had to be hospitalized. She's spent days and nights in emergency rooms, served as a taxi service, counseled squabbling siblings, shopped for clothing and food for clients, and helped to tidy up their homes. Whatever needs to be done, Antony will do it—or find someone else who can.

For example, in 2004 Antony was hired as care manager for an elderly man who'd been severely injured while trying to salvage what was left of his home after a hurricane. While sifting through debris, he fell through a floor and broke his neck. Antony worked with representatives of the Federal Emergency Management Agency to try to get assistance for her client as she dealt with medical personnel, builders, home health care providers, insurance companies, lawyers, doctors, and rehabilitation specialists while trying to secure every possible service for her client. "We had to tap into resources we'd never used before," Antony says. "It was very complex, but very rewarding."

of information, regarding various institutions. The care manager will also have to address financial concerns. In order to do that, the manager needs to have many resources in place.

Because no one can be fully informed on every issue that might arise in a geriatric care situation, it's vitally important that you know where to get the help that you need. That means you have to have a network of dependable resources available, including lawyers, trust officers, nursing home and hospital contacts, transportation providers, and in-home care providers.

A geriatric care manager isn't expected to solve every problem but should certainly know where to go to find the answers. It requires that you be an excellent networker and able to establish good, working relationships with a wide variety of service providers.

Pitfalls

Geriatric care management is difficult, stressful, emotional work, and you'll be expected to be constantly available in case of an emergency. Burnout is not uncommon. All too often you may find yourself in the middle of a family dispute, such as siblings fighting over a parent's money or property. You'll also have to grapple with endless red tape and accept lower wages than experts in other health care areas, such as nursing. And working with the elderly can be emotionally wrenching, as you get to know individuals nearing the end of life; inevitably, some of them will die during the time they're in your care.

Perks

If you enjoy helping people, you'll get enormous satisfaction out of being a geriatric care manager. If you're the type of person who enjoys solving problems, you'll be a natural for this job. The scope of the job varies tremendously, so you'll always be doing something different. Since this job tends to be hands-on, you won't be stuck at a desk all day, either. You'll get to meet a lot of people in many different disciplines, and you're bound to learn a lot along the way about a variety of topics.

Get a Jump on the Job

You can find out whether you like working with older people by spending some time with them. Offer to teach an elderly person how to use a computer, or read to an older person who is visually impaired. Volunteer at a local nursing home or assisted living center, or if you're old enough, apply for a job in the dining room of an assisted living center. Read books about caring for elderly people. Check out the phone list to see what services for elderly people exist in your community and learn what they do. Volunteer to help out at a senior center.

HERPETOLOGIST

OVERVIEW

If you find reptiles and amphibians fascinating and endearing rather than creepy, crawly, and downright icky, then a career as a herpetologist might be for you. Herpetology is the scientific study of reptiles and amphibians. In many ways, a herpetologist's job is a lot like that of paleontologists, entomologists, or ethologists, except that herpetologists deal with snakes, lizards, frogs, alligators, turtles and other reptilian and amphibious creatures.

All herpetologists are first biologists, with a good knowledge of general biology, who have a specialized knowledge of amphibians and reptiles. In fact, herpetology is really a subfield of biology, and jobs in biology traditionally fall into four areas: college and university jobs; state or federal government work; medicine; and zoological parks or museums.

The most desired herpetology jobs involve extensive research doing species population counts, observing general behavior of select animals, conducting food supply studies, and sometimes even searching for new species. But many herpetologists work as another type of scientist and add their herpetologist interest on the side. For example, you might be trained in ecology and conduct environmental impact studies for the government. But if you're also a herpetologist, then you might choose to study reptiles and amphibians as a way of detecting changes in the environment. A medical hematologist might, if also interested in herpetology, study the blood of reptiles and amphibians. Herpetologists

AT A GLANCE

Salary Range

College or university professors earn between $30,000 and $80,000, depending on experience; full-time research or laboratory assistants, $17,000 to $35,000; museum curators and scientists, $30,000 to $80,000; full-time museum assistant positions, $12,000 to $18,000; collection managers, $18,000 to $45,000; zoo curators and supervisors, $30,000 to $50,000; and zookeepers, $15,000 to $25,000.

Education/Experience

You'll need at least a master's degree, but most herpetologists have a Ph.D. A college education with an emphasis in the biological sciences is recommended, since there is no college or university that offers a major in herpetology. Herpetologists should also take courses in statistics, chemistry, computer science, writing, and foreign languages. The school should have a good academic record, be strong in the sciences, and particularly strong in organismal biology. The competition for jobs in herpetology is very intense, so postgraduate studies can be critical to your career.

Personal Attributes

Willingness to stand adverse conditions; a strong interest in one or more kinds of amphibians and reptiles, and the persistence and determination necessary to be successful at doing what you want to do.

Requirements

Excellent research skills with good observation and communication skills, an interest in science.

Outlook

Fair to poor. This is a competitive field where there are more people who study reptiles and amphibians than there are jobs for them. There are not many jobs directly related to herpetology, and you may find it necessary to accept a position removed from your prime area of interest.

may work in zoos or for wildlife agencies, do environmental assessments, teach, or care for museum collections. Some herpetologists work as writers, photographers, or animal breeders.

Most herpetologists, however, labor not in the field, but in the classroom. Working as a professor or researcher in a college or university, the herpetologist is usually expected to teach a variety of biology courses, such as introductory biology, systematics, anatomy, physiology, or ecology, as well as herpetology.

If you don't have a Ph.D., you could land a job as a university research assistant or laboratory assistant, which would allow you to pursue herpetological studies as a sideline in an academic setting, with access to good libraries and research equipment.

Museums offer other jobs for herpetologists. Curators or scientists are usually able to devote most of their time to doing research on amphibians and reptiles. These positions require a Ph.D. in biology. In university-affiliated museums, the jobs of professor and curator are combined, so that one individual both teaches and does museum research.

Collection managers take care of preserved amphibians and reptiles, cataloging specimens, logging records, and making specimens available for research. To be a collection manager, you'll need to have a master's degree in biology or museum studies. With a bachelor's degree, you could work as a full-time museum assistant.

There are several types of herpetological jobs available in zoos; zoo curators and supervisors are manager positions that usually require a master's degree in biology. Most zookeeper jobs require a bachelor's degree (and sometimes a graduate degree) in biology. Zookeepers are primary caregivers for the animals in their charge. Some zoos have positions available as educators (usually requiring a master's degree) or researchers at the Ph.D. level.

There are a few government jobs for herpetologists in wildlife management, usually in nongame programs. Some of these are field positions, others involve work researching and writing regulations. There are also a few jobs for herpetologists with private conservation organizations; you'll need a bachelor's degree in wildlife management, and often a master's degree or Ph.D. in biology.

If you're the independent type, you might want to go into business for yourself breeding and selling amphibians and reptiles, or selling herpetological-related merchandise and publications. A very few people earn a living selling frog legs for food, or extracting snake venom for medical and research use.

It's also possible to make a good living writing books and magazine articles about herpetology, photographing amphibians and reptiles, or making nature films.

Many herpetologists don't have jobs directly related to herpetology, but they're still able to keep herpetology as part of their career focus—these jobs might include high school science teachers, veterinarians, environmental technicians, and biomedical researchers.

Graduate programs at many universities allow you to do advanced studies on some aspects of herpetology, and sometimes a fairly small university may have an outstanding herpetologist on its faculty. One good way to select a university for graduate study is to check out the current issues of the major herpetological journals (*Copeia*, *Herpetologica*, and *Journal of Herpetology*). When you find articles on the kind of research that interests you, check and see where the researchers

Jesus Rivas, herpetologist

Technically a biologist, Jesus Rivas is passionate about natural history and conservation, and has been working for several years studying the behavioral ecology and conservation of large tropical reptiles of the *llanos* (grasslands) of Venezuela, his homeland. "Since I was a little kid I used to love animals," he says. "I wanted to be with them, and learn about them. I used to drive my mother crazy with my questions. Eventually, I studied biology, and one thing followed another."

Although most of his experience has been with green iguanas and green anacondas, he explains, he also worked with other reptiles, such as the Orinoco crocodile, the spectacled caiman, and green sea turtles. At the moment, he's focusing on anacondas, which was the topic of his doctoral dissertation at the University of Tennessee, where he studied at the Laboratory of Reptile Ethology. After graduation, Rivas taught tropical ecology at Boston University, and then started making TV documentaries for National Geographic Television as a field correspondent.

"Working with TV is a fairly demanding activity," he notes, "and it certainly takes a lot of time from scientific activities." But he loves the chance to reach a huge audience with his conservation message. Noting how much he loves teaching, he explains that it's often hard for him to choose between teaching at a school where he can reach just a small number of students, or creating a film that can reach millions. At present, he is teaching tropical ecology at Otterbein College in Columbus, Ohio, which leaves him free to complete documentaries as a freelance filmmaker.

Before he came to the United States to go to school, he worked as a fireman in the inner cities of Venezuela, which taught him that society's problems can't be solved with shortsighted programs that attack just a few aspects of the whole issue. "I am deeply concerned about habitat degradation and human activities that affect the well-being of other animals," he explains. "I am a firm advocate for conservation education at both the early ages and at the college level." He also believes that if humans are to succeed in the campaign for habitat conservation, "it will not be by using a whole lot more of technology, but by using a little bit more of common sense."

Eventually, he hopes he can raise international conservation money to create a nature reserve in the *llanos* and across South America to protect the land from timber industries, oil exploration, and poaching. He'd also like to build a tourist lodge for visitors to appreciate the beauty of the area, and help conserve the land. It would include a research center used for tropical studies and for environmental education.

His advice to young herpetologists is to study animals in local zoos or preserves, but if you must own your own snake, don't buy an exotic species from a pet shop. "Buying an anaconda encourages illegal trade," he says. "Find a local snake instead, and if it escapes, it won't be a problem in the environment. It's good for kids to like animals. This nurtures their love of animals and taking care of other living things. But kids just need to make sure they make the right choices."

Rivas says he prefers to collect original data in the field of wild animals and to look for new trends and new interpretations. Every March and April finds him in South America, doing what he loves best. In fact, he admits that it's hard for him to tell the difference between working and vacation, because he so loves what he does. "I get to go to great places, and interact with the animals I love."

are based, and apply to those institutions. A few universities have had a long tradition of producing herpetologists, including Harvard, Cornell, and the universities of Florida, Michigan, Kansas, and California at Berkeley. Other centers for herpetological study include Duke University, University of Chicago, University of Texas at Austin, and University of Texas at Arlington.

The specific training required for a career in herpetology varies according to what you want to do for a career. A great deal of herpetological research is conducted in other countries and facility in one or more foreign languages allows you to follow such activities in other nations. As in other branches of science, computer literacy is really important, and students should enroll in courses that provide training in computer use.

Pitfalls

Herpetology can be a tough field to break into, and it can be hard to find good jobs.

Perks

If you love these kinds of animals, then finding a job in which you can continue your work with them can be exciting and interesting. Many herpetology-related research or conservation jobs include extensive travel all over the world.

Get a Jump on the Job

Read all of the books and magazine articles you can about these animals. Becoming an active member of a regional herpetological society is a good way to meet others with common interests. Going out to search for amphibians and reptiles is an excellent way to sharpen observation and note-taking skills. Record your field observations of amphibians and reptiles carefully in permanent field books. Learn how to take good photographs of animals and their habitats.

HISTORICAL INTERPRETER

OVERVIEW

What was Ben Franklin like as a child? Who were his parents? Did he have brothers and sisters? When did he first come to Philadelphia? What did he like to eat? What books did he read? Who were his friends? What were his thoughts and opinions about issues? Did he really fly a kite with a key tied onto it during a lightning storm? If you were an historical interpreter for Ben Franklin, you'd have to know all this—and much more.

A good historical interpreter has the ability to leave the 21st century and go back to an earlier place and time in history. A really good historical interpreter has the ability to take the audience along for the ride.

Historical interpreters give their audiences an authentic look at what it was like during a particular period of history as they reenact life during the period, paying attention to the smallest details in order to make their presentation believable. Many historical interpreters work at "living history" sites such as Williamsburg or Jamestown, but there are many other smaller sites, such as restored historic farms and plantations, factories, and battlefields.

If you work at a living history site, you'll be expected to dress in the type of clothing that was worn during the period. You'll cook the same way and eat the same kinds of foods. You'll work the way they did, read the same books, use the same methods of light and heat, go to the same kind of schools (or not), and care for the

AT A GLANCE

Salary Range

A full-time historical interpreter working at a national or state historic site can earn between $18,026 and $57,759 a year, with a median salary of about $31,500. However, many historical interpreters are self-employed and cannot count on a regular salary.

Education/Experience

Requirements vary; some jobs may require a bachelor's degree in history or another area, but there are no standard educational requirements.

Personal Attributes

You should be extremely outgoing and comfortable speaking in front of people. It's very important for historical interpreters to remain in character, so you need to have good concentration skills. Because historical interpreters are actors, it helps if you have some theatrical ability and experience.

Requirements

You must be intimately familiar with whatever period of history you're "living" in, with a real commitment to study and learn all you can about the details of a historical period.

Outlook

Good. More jobs are expected to open in the field of historical interpretation as the number of museums and historic sites around the country continues to increase.

same types of animals. In short, you'll be expected to conform as closely to the lives of the original inhabitants as possible. In order to do that, of course, you have to know a lot about the time period you'll be "living" in, and all that you can learn about the person you'll be portraying. For that portrayal of Benjamin Franklin, for instance, you'd have to know everything possible about his life because your audience expects you to be Ben Franklin.

Fortunately, there's a lot of information available about most major historical characters, making it easy for you to learn about them. The question is, how hard would you be willing to work? The more you know, the more convincing your char-

---

Michael T. Francis, historical interpreter

Mike Francis considers himself a lucky guy. Portraying Galileo, the Italian court mathematician credited with major celestial discoveries in the 17th century, gives him the opportunity to combine his love of science with his love of acting. That combination, Francis thinks, is a winner.

"Anyone who wants to excel in historical interpretation must master both the history and the craft," Francis says. With three physics degrees, experience as a physical science and physics teacher, and 10 years experience as a lecturer at the Charles Hayden Planetarium at the Museum of Science in Boston, Francis is well equipped to handle the scientific aspects of portraying the famous astronomer and mathematician. His extensive experience in film, video, and theater provide him with the skills to play a very convincing Galileo in programs he presents at schools, libraries, and museums.

Francis, who lives in Auburndale, Massachusetts, finds that his career move toward becoming a historical interpreter was a natural one. "I worked at the Charles Hayden Planetarium as a lecturer and photographer for 10 years, while I also worked in numerous plays, TV programs, and films," Francis says. "When I left the planetarium, I decided I wanted to continue using my experience in both astronomy and acting. My friend Jim Cooke, who portrays Calvin Coolidge, had been combining his love of history with theater, so I decided to try my own variation."

Why Galileo?

"Galileo, being the father of modern astronomy, seemed the logical choice," Francis says. "After I began digging deeper and learning more about him and his life, he became the only choice."

Francis performs around the Boston area, but also has traveled to New Mexico, Michigan, Ohio, Pennsylvania, New York, Vermont, Connecticut, Rhode Island, New Hampshire, and South Carolina to portray Galileo at schools and organizations.

He gets the word out about his act by mailing information once a year to all elementary and middle schools in Massachusetts, New Hampshire, and Rhode Island. He also has a Web site (http://www.gis.net/~mtf) that highlights his performances, and he relies on satisfied customers to pass along the word about his performance.

When Francis portrays Galileo to students, he begins by giving a lecture on the most recent discoveries he's made while using his telescope. "Galileo was quite a lecturer himself," Francis says. "He used humor and lively demonstrations to present his findings, so it makes for a rather entertaining presentation. "After the lecture, Francis meets with students and teachers to give them a chance to ask him questions about the life and times of the famous astronomer.

"I work very hard to never break character when I'm with my audience," he says. "And I don't think I ever have. I don't even like it when people introduce me to the audience as Mike Francis, portraying Galileo. They should introduce me as Galileo only."

acter will be, and the more adept you'll become at historical interpretation.

Some historical interpreters work as tour guides at historical sites such as Colonial Williamsburg, while others demonstrate traditional crafts, such as blacksmithing and candle making. Still other interpreters portray regular people in their daily lives, doing chores such as cooking and chopping wood. Historical interpreters also act in historical plays and participate in reenactments, such as battles or encampments.

Pitfalls

Much of this work is seasonal, making it difficult in some cases to earn enough money. Many historical interpreters work at other jobs in addition to interpreting. Historical interpretation jobs that are funded with government money are always in danger of being eliminated if the economy declines.

Perks

Most historical interpreters love their jobs, which makes them lots of fun to be around.

If you have an outgoing personality, a real interest in history, as well as a love of acting, being a historical interpreter is probably a job that you'll love.

Get a Jump on the Job

The best thing you can do to begin preparing for a job as a historical interpreter is to become as familiar as possible with the historical period in which you're interested. If you have your heart set on portraying a Civil War doctor, for instance, read everything you can about the Civil War, concentrating on medical information. Then start looking for opportunities to talk to others about what you've learned. By the time you're in high school, you may be able to volunteer as an interpreter at a living history site near your home. Many historical sites offer internship positions to high school or college students.

HOSPITAL CHAPLAIN

OVERVIEW

While hospital chaplains are sometimes overlooked, they play an important role in the life of the institution and in the care and support of its patients. Hospital chaplains perform a variety of tasks and duties, but their primary responsibility is to tend to the spiritual, emotional, and religious needs of patients, their families, and hospital staff members.

Hospitals are not the only institutions that hire and utilize chaplains. Mental health facilities, nursing homes, and prisons also provide chaplains to counsel and minister to patients, residents, and inmates.

While most chaplains are affiliated with a particular faith, a hospital chaplain must be available to all patients, regardless of their religious beliefs or affiliations. There are chaplains who are Jewish, Muslim, and Christian, with many variations within those main religions.

Regardless of their own faith, chaplains are expected to provide the same service to patients of every belief and faith. Chaplains do not seek to convert patients, simply to serve their spiritual needs in whatever manner possible.

A hospital chaplain might pray with a patient, read from a holy book, talk about how the patient is feeling, or simply sit with a patient. He or she also works with families of patients who are suffering through the illness or even death of a loved one. The chaplain sometimes counsels families forced to make very difficult decisions con-

AT A GLANCE

Salary Range

The average salary for a hospital chaplain ranges between $40,000 and $56,000, depending on the size and location of the hospital and other factors.

Education/Experience

Most hospitals require chaplains to have both a bachelor's degree and a master's of divinity degree. In addition, you'll need a year of specialized training, which is known as the Clinical Pastoral Education program, and must work as a resident before becoming fully certified as a hospital chaplain.

Personal Attributes

You should be compassionate, concerned, and caring, and not afraid to be around people who are dealing with extremely tough issues, including death and dying. Although it's important to be able to empathize with patients and their families, you can't be the type of person who falls apart and becomes emotionally distraught because people will be looking to you for strength and comfort. You must be comfortable in a hospital setting, able to communicate well with others, and able to treat all people—regardless of their faith or other factors—with respect and love.

Requirements

Some hospitals, but not all, require their chaplains to be ordained ministers. Chaplains must be certified by professional organizations.

Outlook

The outlook for hospital chaplain positions is strong, due to an increasing number of aging Americans and an emerging trend for hospitals to focus on a more holistic treatment for patients, paying attention to the needs of mind, body, and soul.

cerning end-of-life issues for a loved one. He or she might stay with a dying patient who has no family available, provide pre- or postsurgical counseling, lead a memorial service, provide grief counseling, or work to support a family in crisis due to illness or other misfortune. Chaplains also provide support for staff members struggling with spiritual or emotional issues.

Working as a hospital chaplain often is very difficult. Shorter hospital stays mean that chaplains sometimes must connect

Rev. Gregory A. Stoddard, hospital chaplain

Rev. Gregory A. Stoddard has been a hospital chaplain for many years, and still marvels over the great variety of work the job entails.

He many times has been roused from sleep and requested to come quickly to the emergency room to be with the family of a person who had been seriously or critically injured. He visits patients in their hospital rooms, working with them to get them through tough times. He counsels medical staff in times of trouble, such as after the 9/11 attacks. He participates on the hospital's ethics committee, is part of its trauma team, and prays at the dedications of new buildings and staff dinners. He, or a member of his staff, is called every time there is a death within the hospital to pray with and provide counsel to family members.

At the forefront of all his work as director of chaplaincy services at Reading Hospital in West Reading, Pennsylvania, however, is to at all times represent the hospital's commitment to compassionate care.

"I think of the chaplain at Reading Hospital as being the clearest representation that we have to our commitment to compassionate care," Stoddard said. "Compassion is to have a deep empathy for what people are going through. That is a high order for a health care facility where everyone is as busy as they are here. It's the job of the chaplains to convey that care to all patients and their families."

In order to do that, Stoddard and his staff talk with and listen to patients who are in pain, who are doubting their faith, and who are scared of what lies ahead. They provide a quiet, reassuring presence in the midst of the turmoil and anguish that is an unavoidable part of the life of a hospital.

Stoddard said hospital chaplains work very hard at being accepting and affirming of people from all faiths and walks of life. It doesn't matter if a patient is a community business leader or an addict who's been shot during a drug dispute, both of them receive the same respect from the chaplaincy staff.

The work of a hospital chaplain can be draining, but Stoddard said there is no regular turnover of chaplaincy staff at his hospital. Instead, he said, the chaplains there take heart from the inspiring people they meet.

"The job can be very difficult, but it doesn't really overwhelm," Stoddard said. "There's actually a pretty remarkable sense of satisfaction and accomplishment."

When asked to describe the work of a hospital chaplain, Stoddard put it this way.

"I tell people that if they saw it on the front page of their local newspaper, there was a chaplain involved. But, you'll never read on that front page that the chaplain was involved, and that's okay. That's just the way it should be."

with patients outside of the hospital setting. There are meetings to attend, paperwork to complete, and the ever-present task of supporting people whose lives have been turned upside down.

The services of a hospital chaplain are vitally important, and will become increasingly important as attention turns to treating the "whole" patient instead of just the physical illness.

Pitfalls

Being a hospital chaplain requires a significant educational investment, which means a commitment of time and financial resources. The work of a chaplain can be pretty much continuously physically, mentally, and emotionally draining, as it requires that you, in some sense, experience the pain and suffering of the patient you're serving. You may work long hours, and must be prepared at times to respond quickly to the needs of patients and their families.

Perks

Helping someone get to the other side of a bleak or seemingly hopeless period in their lives can be extremely rewarding. Hospital chaplains generally get great satisfaction from caring for patients, and patients and their families are generally appreciative of the efforts of chaplains.

Get a Jump on the Job

Volunteer at a nursing home or hospital so that you'll have an opportunity to get used to being around people who are ill. See if you might be able to arrange a meeting with a chaplain from your local hospital to ask questions about what the job entails. Begin studying theology and learn about the different religions of the world and the beliefs and practices of the people who adhere to those religions.

HYPNOTHERAPIST

OVERVIEW

Mention hypnosis and most people think about the guy in front of the college audience making participants quack like a duck or eat a raw potato. Actually, that type of hypnosis is really more entertainment than science—but hypnosis does have a place in the treatment of real problems, both physical and mental.

Most therapeutic hypnotists are psychologists who use hypnosis as an additional help in working with clients overcoming a variety of problems. Hypnosis can be a very helpful psychological tool if it is properly and ethically administered. Studies show that hypnosis can treat everything from chronic pain to poor study habits. For example, a psychologist might use hypnosis as part of a treatment plan to control symptoms such as anxiety, panic attacks, or phobias. Therapeutic hypnotists also use hypnosis to help clients break negative habits, such as overeating or smoking, or to reinforce positive mental attitudes. Finally, hypnosis can be very effective in helping some clients manage pain.

Most professionals would define hypnosis as a very deep state of relaxation in which your mind is focused. Hypnosis isn't some kind of magical voodoo that will turn you into someone you aren't, or that will make you do anything against your ethical beliefs. What it can do is help you to focus on specific areas of your life with more clarity and teach you how to face life in a positive manner. A hypnotist is an entertainer—the guy you see up on stage trying to get you to cluck like a duck.

AT A GLANCE

Salary Range

$37,490 to more than $87,060, depending on type of practice and specialty.

Education/Experience

Unfortunately, in most states anyone can call himself or herself a hypnotist or hypnotherapist by taking a correspondence course or paying a fee. Although it is easy to learn how to induce hypnosis, it takes a lot of psychological training to apply hypnosis effectively, safely, and ethically. Ideally, you should have a Ph.D. in psychology or a master's in social work (M.S.W.) from an accredited university. In most states, psychologists and social workers are licensed.

Personal Attributes

You must be emotionally stable, mature, and able to deal effectively with people. Sensitivity, compassion, good communication skills, patience, and perseverance are vital qualities. A soothing voice is also helpful.

Requirements

Hypnotherapists who are psychologists in independent practice or those who offer any type of patient care—including clinical, counseling, and school psychologists and social workers—must meet certification or licensing requirements in all states and must pass an exam. Licensing laws vary by state and by type of position. Clinical and counseling psychologists usually require a doctorate in psychology, completion of an approved internship, and one or two years of professional experience. Most states certify those with a master's degree as school psychologists after completion of an internship. Some states require continuing education for license renewal.

Outlook

Good; the job outlook for health care professionals using hypnotherapy is expected to grow faster than

(continues)

A hypnotherapist and a hypnotist are quite different.

As a hypnotherapist, you'll use hypnosis as part of a treatment plan to help your clients get well, break a habit, or improve their lifestyle. Most people can be hypnotized, although some people more easily reach that state than others. This may depend on the person's belief in hypnosis, trust in the therapist, how safe the person feels, how well he can concentrate, and a quiet, peaceful environment. The key to helping a client reach a hypnotic state is to help the person relax and focus on the body

Tom Kersting, Ph.D., hypnotherapist

Tom Kersting was a pitcher on his college baseball team when he discovered the power of hypnosis. In the middle of a slump, he couldn't seem to strike anybody out anymore.

"Self-doubt crept in and made me believe my skills had disappeared and that I'd never be able to pitch effectively again," he recalls. That same year, a pitcher for the Atlanta Braves solved the same problem by working with a sports psychologist and hypnotherapist, who taught him how to free himself from his mental rut. "When I heard his story," Kersting says, "I decided to give hypnosis a try, although I was pretty skeptical." After just two sessions, Kersting made a complete turnaround, too. "The negative, crippling thoughts disappeared and I became immersed in positive, productive thoughts," he says. "I became fascinated with the power of the mind."

He ended up changing his major to psychology, eventually earning a master's degree in counseling and human development, a second master's in administration and supervision, and then a Ph.D. in clinical hypnotherapy.

Today he's in private practice in northern New Jersey, using hypnotherapy to help patients lose weight, stop smoking, and embrace exercise. "I always try to implement hypnosis with clients," he says, "because a lot of things that are preventing people from moving forward are beyond consciousness. Hypnotherapy is a good way of helping them awaken their strengths and abilities. Traditional talk therapy doesn't always do that."

Kersting has been practicing hypnosis since 2001, although he's been doing hypnosis and researching the subject since 1991. He got his degree in clinical hypnotherapy from American Pacific University, but he warns students interested in hypnotherapy that they may find a hard time getting trained in hypnosis as part of a traditional clinical psychology program. "You'll learn about hypnosis in those programs," he says, "but you won't learn hypnosis." Typically, the subject is included in a theory course, but doesn't really focus on using hypnosis in counseling. "I think our country is still very traditional," he explains.

and mind. Without these hypnosis will not work, at least not as well as possible. Of course, it's not a matter of being hypnotized or not—the hypnotic state actually exists on a continuum. Most people can be hypnotized to some degree—the only question is how deeply they'll descend into the hypnotic state.

Of course, a client won't change behavior or break a habit just as a result of being hypnotized. Rather, once the client is hypnotized, the therapist offers specific suggestions and images that reach the client on a subconscious level, which can actually alter their behavior as he or she rehearses new ways to act or think while in trance. For example, during hypnosis, a therapist may tell a client trying to quit smoking that hours will pass without the person thinking about smoking, and that if he takes a cigarette, it will taste terrible. The therapist then explores with the hypnotized client what being a nonsmoker would feel—how fresh the air will smell,

To Kersting, combining hypnosis with psychotherapy just makes common sense—and the results can be evident quickly. "You can never promote hypnotherapy as a cure-all," he cautions. "You never want to promote it as a one-shot thing where you get hypnotized and you're cured; but immediate cures do happen. In general, it's something that needs to be practiced over time." However, he finds the quick response some people experience to be gratifying. "I had a woman in my office last week who was a bundle of stress and nerves," he says. "When she came in this week I could sense she was much calmer and relaxed, more focused and composed. You can really see it."

About half his clients seek hypnotherapy for weight loss, although he uses the techniques for a variety of other situations. In fact, he's found hypnotherapy to be such a powerful tool in weight loss and exercise that he's just completed a book about self-hypnosis and weight loss published by Harbor Press.

Although Kersting loves his job, he does get frustrated with the fact that so few people really understand the true nature of the techniques. "Probably 90 percent of people who come in always associate it with things they've seen on TV and in the movies," he says. "They don't understand the therapeutic use of hypnosis. They see it as hocus pocus." They come to him, he says, hoping that hypnotherapy will be a quick fix. "But it's not magic. I explain it to them and really go over it with them. Students who are interested in being a hypnotherapist should first get training and a license in psychology or counseling, he stresses. "There aren't too many guidelines for hypnosis. You can take weekend courses and get certified, but you really need a background in psychology to do counseling." Kersting recommends students check into two major organizations: the American Institute of Hypnosis and the National Guild of Hypnosis, which offer three levels of training.

"I love my work, and helping patients see real results so quickly," he says. "And I like introducing them to their own healing process."

how good food will taste, and so on. In addition, the deep relaxation a client experiences during a hypnotic trance can be very beneficial on both a physical and psychological level.

Pitfalls

It can sometimes be difficult to have insurance companies reimburse treatment for hypnosis alone.

Perks

Helping clients conqueror their fears, break bad habits, and live happier, healthier lives is an incredible boost to anyone interested in working in the mental health or holistic fields.

Get a Jump on the Job

Read everything you can about hypnosis, and learn how to perform self-hypnosis. Then study hard—lots of science and math—and plan to spend many years studying to become a health or mental health professional.

LAUGHTER THERAPIST

OVERVIEW

The average person laughs 17 times a day—and the more guffaws, the better for your health, since researchers estimate that laughing 100 times is equal to 10 minutes on the rowing machine or 15 minutes on an exercise bike. In fact, the medical and spiritual benefits of laughing are so apparent that an entire medical field has evolved to take advantage of its benefits: laughter therapy.

As the years pass, laughter therapy is becoming more widely accepted as a supplemental treatment for many disorders, designed to make existing treatments work better. Once looked upon with suspicion, laughter therapists are becoming much more accepted by mainstream medicine.

It's not the job of a laughter therapist to stand up in front of a group of people and crack jokes, show funny pictures, or do tricks to make people laugh. A laughter therapist teaches people how to look for and recognize humor in the everyday occurrences of life, encouraging clients to take themselves a little less seriously and create more occasions for laughter. If you've ever watched the movie *Patch Adams*, based on the life work of the doctor Hunter "Patch" Adams, who used humor and laughter to improve healing in his patients, you've seen laughter therapy in action.

Laughter therapy is based on some of the same properties as yoga, in that it works to make you aware of your motions and actions. While methods of laughter therapy vary, many therapists lead groups

AT A GLANCE

Salary Range

The average salary of a laughter therapist is $26,900, according to government statistics. However, salaries fluctuate depending on hours, setting, and location. Most laughter therapists work only part time while holding other jobs.

Education/Experience

There are no specific educational requirements to be a laughter therapist. Many are trained counselors or have medical backgrounds and take training in laughter therapy as an addition to their education. People specialize in laughter therapy from a wide range of backgrounds, including social work, physical therapy, yoga, the arts, and psychology. Several organizations, such as the World Laughter Tour, train and certify people as laughter therapists. You can find out more about the World Laughter Tour in Appendix A.

Personal Attributes

You don't have to be a stand-up comedian to be a laughter therapist, but it certainly helps if you have a good sense of humor and you get along well with other people. You should have excellent communication skills and good natural speaking ability. You'll spend a lot of time in front of people, and some of the exercises that laughter therapists use in order to engage their audiences can be pretty silly and goofy looking, so it helps if you're not a person who is overly self-conscious or easily embarrassed.

Requirements

Your state may require certification as a laughter therapist. Other requirements will vary depending on your employer and your work situation.

Outlook

Jobs for therapists are expected to increase at a rate that is faster than the national average, increasing between 21 and 35 percent between now and 2012.

in exercises in which the participants clap their hands and chant syllables, words, or other repetitive sounds.

Because laughter is contagious, laughter therapy works well in group settings. Some businesses, including large corporations such as IBM and General Motors, and government agencies such as the FBI and CIA, have hired laughter therapists to conduct workshops for employees. Experts suspect that employees experience less stress and are more productive when laughter therapy is used. In India, "laughter clubs" are common in workplaces, schools, and community events to relieve stress and boost moods.

In addition to reducing stress, laughter therapy has been medically proven to

Susan Magee-Bibi, laughter therapist

Susan Magee-Bibi wasn't in a laughing mood when she began training to be a laughter therapist in October 2001, just a month after the terrorist attacks on New York City and Washington, D.C. She'd already signed up for the training, however, so she traveled about an hour from her home in Temple, Pennsylvania, to the university offering the course.

Once there, she met Steve Wilson, a psychiatrist, psychoanalyst, and founder of The World Laughter Tour, Inc., who assured her and the other participants that laughter was necessary. "He told us it was okay for us to laugh. In fact, he says that we really needed to laugh," Magee-Bibi says.

Magee-Bibi went ahead with the training, eventually becoming certified as a laughter therapist. Now she presents laughter club sessions to groups in her area, during which she introduces them to the benefits of laughing and leads them in exercises meant to induce laughter. "It's not joke telling or anything like that," Magee-Bibi says. "Laughter therapy is actually a form of yoga. Laughter club is a time when you give yourself permission to laugh, just for the joy of laughing."

As far as Magee-Bibi is concerned, people in general don't laugh hard enough or often enough. "I really think we take ourselves too seriously these days," she says. "We don't take time to laugh, or we don't laugh simply because we don't let ourselves."

Once you give yourself permission to laugh, you'll begin looking for—and finding—reasons to, Magee-Bibi says. "Once you start laughing you'll really feel good," she says. "You'll wonder why you didn't start years ago."

One of the most important things about laughter therapy, is that it encourages only laughter that is healthy and positive. "It's not laughter that's at someone else's expense or negative in any way," Magee-Bibi says. "It's just healthy, make-you-feel-good laughter. Anyone can do it, and everyone can benefit from it."

Magee-Bibi is the youth services coordinator for her county's public library system and works part time as a laughter therapist. She first got involved with training to be a laughter therapist because she wanted to do a library summer program with a humor theme. Now she can't imagine her life without the laughter clubs.

"It's been great, and people have been really receptive," she says. "But, why wouldn't they be? Who doesn't like to laugh?"

help lower blood pressure, increase muscle function, boost the immune system, help control pain, and produce a general sense of well-being.

Pitfalls

Laughter therapy is one unusual job most people have never heard of, so jobs may remain somewhat limited until they do. You may need to do a lot of marketing work to let people know about laughter therapy and promote it as a valuable service.

Perks

What could be more fun than making people laugh and feel better about life? Laughter therapists generally find their

work to be very rewarding—and fun. Because most laughter therapists have been trained to find laughter and fun in their lives, that tends to make them happier, healthier, and more well balanced.

Get a Jump on the Job

Check out the Web sites of the Humor Project, Inc. and the World Laughter Tour (see Appendix A). You may be able to find a laughter club or an opportunity to attend a laughter therapist training session in your area. Read books about laughter therapy and look for reasons to laugh and tune into how you feel when you do. Think about keeping a journal that notes how you feel before and after a good laugh.

MASSAGE THERAPIST

OVERVIEW

Using only a bottle of scented oil, your hands, a massage table, and maybe a few candles or soothing music, you can work magic on the tired aching muscles of your clients and make a nice living, all without even leaving your home.

As a professional massage therapist, you'd provide healing treatments by manipulating soft body tissue and muscles, using your hands, sometimes your elbows, and occasionally even your feet. Massage therapy is used to help relieve stress and pain, reduce blood pressure, and boost the immune system. The most popular types of therapy include Swedish massage, the most common type of massage designed to relax and energize the client; deep tissue massage, which treats muscle damage from an injury, such as whiplash or back strain; or sports massage, which can help prevent sports injuries, keep the athlete flexible, and heal the body if an injury occurs.

Most massage therapists specialize in one type of massage, although many offer a variety of treatments. Some combine massage with other aspects of beauty and complementary therapy. Other types of treatments may include aromatherapy, Indian head massage, shiatsu, foot reflexology, or lymphatic drainage. It also may involve chair massage (a massage of the upper body, while the client is fully clothed and seated in a special portable chair).

As a massage therapist, you may work in a health spa, cruise ship, clinic, fitness center, hospital, wellness center, doctor's

AT A GLANCE

Salary Range

$15,899 to $35,332; self-employed massage therapists may earn more than $70,660.

Education/Experience

Most applicants study for a one- or two-year full-time course at a college or private massage school before getting a job. The American Massage Therapy Association recommends a minimum of 500 hours of in-class training, including a specified number of hours in anatomy and physiology, the theory and practice of massage therapy, and elective subjects. Training programs that are accredited by the Commission on Massage Training Accreditation offer a minimum of 500 in-class hours of training in required subjects and have the faculty, staff, equipment, classrooms, and other attributes needed to provide adequate training in massage therapy.

Personal Attributes

Able to work in close contact with clients, capable of carrying out extended physical activity, interest in people.

Requirements

Training in massage therapy. Thirty-three states and the District of Columbia regulate massage therapists, requiring minimum standards. Each state law is different and has different requirements, so a massage therapist may be referred to as licensed, state certified, or registered. In those states that regulate therapeutic massage, only those individuals who have the state designation may perform massage and use a title indicating that person does massage.

In addition, massage therapists can take an exam to be certified by the National Certification Board for Therapeutic Massage and Bodywork (NCBTMB). To be eligible to sit for the exam, candidates must have completed at least 100 hours of anatomy/physiology; at least 200 hours of massage and/or bodywork theory and application; and at least 200 hours of related coursework. The NCBTMB

AT A GLANCE

certification program includes practitioners of Swedish massage, shiatsu, polarity therapy, Rolfing, Trager techniques, reflexology, and neuromuscular therapy. If you pass the exam and meet standards of education, training, and/or experience, you're entitled to use the designation Nationally Certified in Therapeutic Massage and Bodywork and the initials, NCTMB.

Outlook

Good. This field is expected to continue to expand through 2012.

office, corporation, professional sports organization, or in private practice. A full-time massage therapist in a beauty salon or a spa typically works a regular schedule, between 37 and 40 hours a week, including some weekends and nights. If you're self-employed, however, your hours will depend on how many bookings you choose to take and your client list.

Today, more than 80,000 nationally certified practitioners serve millions of consumers. Nationally certified practitioners are at work in a number of capacities—in physicians' offices, private practices, health clubs, fitness centers, spas, and hospitals.

Karen Wenrich, massage therapist

Pennsylvania massage therapist Karen Wenrich had been interested in massage therapy for many years but never had the opportunity to take a class until a friend suggested they take a class together. The two went for one-on-one training at the Pennsylvania School of Muscle Therapy. "I went for Swedish massage training for three months," Wenrich says, "and then I went back four years later for a nine-month program of more intense training, which did more with anatomy, physiology, pathology, and technique." She specialized in Swedish and deep muscle therapy, and some myofascial release.

Wenrich notices the effect of massage therapy in particular on the circulatory system and on blood pressure. "I've also done some pregnancy massages, some sports massage, and work on cancer patients," she says. "It also can help with rheumatoid arthritis, but you have to be careful if the client is in a highly inflamed state when you're working on them."

Wenrich recommends that students who think they might like to make massage a career should first visit a massage therapist themselves. "They should get bodywork done to see if they would care to be doing that kind of work," she says, "to make sure they're going to like touching people, being in that environment." The next step would be to research potential schools to make sure they attend a good program, she advises. Accreditation is the key thing to look for, she says. Graduating from an accredited school is particularly important if you decide to get more training in a related field, she says.

Very much a part-time therapist who sets her own hours and works out of her home, Wenrich sees about 10 clients a week. "I find it very physically demanding for me," she says. "Upper body mechanics for the therapist is really important. I need to be very mindful how I position myself, how I use my hands," she says.

"I like helping other people," she says, "making them feel better. And I like the flexibility that it gives me in my work schedule."

Consumers who travel can feel confident using the services of a nationally certified practitioner whose practices are aligned with a national standard.

Pitfalls

Massage therapy can be hard physical work, tiring the muscles and joints of your hands, fingers, wrists, and entire upper body.

Perks

If you enjoy working with people and like to help others, massage therapy can pro-vide great job satisfaction. It's also a very portable job: If you have a few basic items plus a massage table, you can set up shop right in your own home and keep your own hours.

Get a Jump on the Job

If you're interested in massage therapy, study all of the biology and anatomy you can and read books about relaxation techniques and massage. Have some bodywork done yourself, so you can see whether this is something you might like to do for a living.

MEDICAL AESTHETICIAN

OVERVIEW

When you go to a dermatologist's office, the white-coated expert applying those cooling lotions and soothing packs is likely a medical aesthetician (also called a para-medical aesthetician or a skin care special-ist). You'll typically find an aesthetician working for licensed health care provid-ers, including plastic surgeons and derma-tologists, providing pre- and postoperative skin care treatment.

Medical aestheticians treat facial skin to maintain and improve its appearance. They often work in offices with derma-tologists, treating patients with problem skin or those whose skin or appearance is affected by trauma or medical procedure, such as surgery. Some work in cancer cen-ters or hospitals. They also may cleanse and beautify the skin by giving facials, full-body treatments, and head and neck massages, and by removing hair through waxing.

Medical aestheticians under the super-vision of a dermatologist may perform exfoliation or other procedures, such as microdermabrasion, use of cosmetics and skin bleaching agents, along with mild skin peels and laser hair and vein removal. Medical aestheticians are also skilled at camouflage makeup. Those who work in burn units might teach burn-recovery patients how to apply makeup to con-ceal their injuries. The aesthetician also is a vital part of the successful outcome of

AT A GLANCE

Salary Range

Average earnings are $22,450, plus tips to $35,240, and many receive commissions on the products they sell. In addition, some salons pay bonuses to employees who bring in new business.

Education/Experience

Training requirements for aestheticians differ by state; aestheticians typically complete a program in skin care at an approved school, usually one that is regulated by the state's board of cosmetology. Program quality varies, so each student should investigate schools' curriculums. Most aesthetician training is general; specialties may require additional education or on-the-job training.

Personal Attributes

Should enjoy working with the public and be willing and able to follow clients' instructions. Communication, image, and attitude play an important role in career success.

Requirements

Licensing, certification, and continuing education requirements for aestheticians differ by state, and many states require a licensing examination for skin care specialists.

Outlook

Overall employment is projected to grow about as fast as the average for all occupations through 2012, because of increasing population, incomes, and demand for personal appearance services. Job openings will occur as workers retire or leave the career; as a result, job opportunities generally should be good. However, competition is expected for jobs at higher paying salons as applicants compete with a large pool of licensed and experienced skin care specialists for these positions. Opportunities will be best for licensed medical aestheticians.

Joyce Pezzulo, medical aesthetician

Joyce Pezzulo was a former electrologist who says she was "always interested" in aesthetics, and that she sort of fell into it because, well, hair and skin just kind of go together. Today, she's the manager of Skin Care Aesthetics of Chestnut Hill, Pennsylvania, and sees a full schedule of patients every day. Pezzulo handles glycolic acid peels, cleansing, microdermabrasions, light treatments, and laser hair removals. In addition, the physicians in the practice might call her in for a consultation. Pezzulo also offers three major lines of cosmetic products.

Medical aesthetics is a very popular field right now, she explains, because everyone wants to look youthful. "Most aestheticians are serious about their jobs," she explains, "and they want to be part of a medical facility where they can be part of an institution instead of independent contractor. There's just a more serious atmosphere. Constant interaction with doctors, getting cutting edge info."

Pezzulo suggests that students interested in aesthetics should "broaden their horizons" and takes lots of science classes, including simple biology or chemistry classes. "That will help you understand the skin itself, the physiology of it," she explains. Pezzulo graduated from the School for Medical Aesthetics in Massachusetts.

"I like my job," Pezzulo says. "It's rewarding, and there's a constant interaction with the public. It's rewarding to see the results that people are looking for."

plastic surgery, especially in the areas of ongoing skincare and postsurgical care.

You'll also find aestheticians working in hospitals, laser centers, salons, medical spas, and retail centers. Aestheticians provide preventive care for the skin and offer treatments to keep the skin healthy and attractive.

Pitfalls

Working as a medical aesthetician can involve long hours on your feet, dealing with the public.

Perks

Most people in this field truly enjoy helping others and making others look and feel better about themselves through better skin care.

Get a Jump on the Job

If you're interested in the field of medical aesthetics, take biology and anatomy courses (as much as you can). You'll also want to read up on and study the skin, cosmetics, and skin care. Consider going to a spa and having some skin treatments done, so you know what a typical visit might be like.

MEDICAL ILLUSTRATOR

OVERVIEW

If you love art and science, and the thought of spending a lot of time exploring various organs way up close doesn't bother you, you might want to consider a career in medical illustration. Medical illustrators combine drawing skills with a detailed knowledge of biology, anatomy, and medicine, which enables them to draw illustrations of human anatomy and surgical procedures. The illustrations are used in medical and scientific publications and in audiovisual presentations for teaching purposes. Medical illustrators also work for lawyers, producing exhibits for court cases.

In the early 20th century, a few medical artists worked as freelancers for medical consultants, hospitals, and medical schools. Most of them had strayed into this area of art by accident. At the end of World War I, a few artists were hired by medical institutions, but it wasn't until the end of World War II that more and more medical artists were hired—so many that hospitals began to establish departments of medical art. As the demand for medical illustrations rose, more and more departments were established. At first, the medical artists' work had centered on anatomical, surgical, and pathological illustrations, but gradually their work began to include more scientific and research work.

Today, in this era of instant digital art, there's still a need for these specialized artists because medical illustrators are the best able to stay current with the changing field. For example, a physician who may

AT A GLANCE

Salary Range

Average starting salary at an institution is between $40,000 and $45,000 a year; experienced salaried illustrators can earn between $45,000 and $75,000; administrators and faculty members generally earn somewhat more. Salaries for freelancers average about $50,000, ranging from $30,000 to more than $120,000. In addition to earnings from a salary or freelance projects, some medical artists have royalty and re-use arrangements with publishers and clients that can provide an additional, and sometimes significant, source of income. Earnings vary significantly according to the experience and ability of the artist, the type of work, and the area of the country.

Education/Experience

A four-year bachelor's degree combining art and premedical courses is preferred; a master's degree in medical illustration (usually a master of science, sometimes a master of art) from an accredited graduate program in medical illustration is recommended. There are currently five such accredited programs in the United States and one in Canada (see Appendix C), each accepting between 3 and 12 students each year. Certification is optional. Medical illustrators can be certified by the Board of Certification of Medical Illustrators if they have passed examinations dealing with business practices, ethics, biomedical science, and drawing skills, and have undergone a rigorous portfolio review. The CMI credential is maintained through meeting continuing education requirements.

Personal Attributes

Artistic ability, interest in science, patience, attention to detail; writing, research, and computer skills are also valuable.

Requirements

Artistic ability and a detailed knowledge of living organisms, surgical and medical procedures, and human and animal anatomy.

(continues)

79

AT A GLANCE *(continued)*

Outlook

Good. This is in part due to the relatively few medical illustrators who graduate each year, and in part due to the growth in medical research that continually requires medical illustrations. Moreover, a growing demand by patients to better understand their own bodies and medical options has boosted the need for medical illustrations aimed at the lay public. Further, greater need for medical illustrations and models to educate juries during courtroom presentations has expanded the forensic subspecialty of medical illustration. On the other hand, the number of medical illustrator positions at medical schools and hospitals is dropping quite fast. Consequently, competition for both salaried and freelance jobs is expected to be keen.

want to illustrate an article or book might ask an artist to draw two different views of the heart, illustrating two separate problems. It's much easier to ask an illustrator to conceptualize this than to try to find actual photos of the problem.

You'll find medical illustrations in a lot more places than in medical textbooks—this work is also used to illustrate medical advertisements, professional journals, instructional videotapes and films, computer-assisted learning programs, exhibits, lecture presentations, general magazines, and programs for television. Although most medical illustrations are used for print and projection media, medical illustrators also work in three dimensions, creating anatomical teaching models, models for simulated medical procedures, and prosthetic parts for patients.

Some medical illustrators specialize in a particular facet of medicine, such as forensic reconstruction, ophthalmologic illustration, medical-legal presentations, or the making of prostheses, often earning considerable recognition for their knowledge and abilities. Other illustrators become an important part of a medical research team. Many illustrators are authors and co-authors of textbooks, or of articles in which they have made major contributions. Experienced medical illustrators may also begin their own businesses, head a group of illustrators or become a director of an audiovisual department.

You'll never be bored as a medical illustrator. Because of the variety of assignments, you'll need to be good at a wide range of art techniques, including drawing, painting, and modeling techniques, as well as the basic concepts and techniques involved in producing commercial and graphic art. A strong foundation in the basic sciences is just as important, so you'll be able to understand and conceptualize complex medical relationships. You'll also need strong visualization skills so you can transform complex information into two-dimensional and three-dimensional images.

Those interested in medical illustration need to be comfortable both working alone and in teams, and also must be able to work closely with clients. You'll need to learn how to figure out not just what the project requires, but your client's often unspoken needs as well.

Many medical illustrators work in medical schools and large medical centers with teaching and research programs. Other medical artists are employed by hospitals, clinics, dental schools, or schools of veterinary medicine. Some institutional medical illustrators work alone, whereas others are part of large multimedia departments. Some medical illustrators choose to target specific markets such as medical publishers, pharmaceutical companies and advertising agencies, physicians or attorneys. Some work independently on a freelance basis; others set up small companies designed to provide illustration services to various targeted markets.

Pitfalls

The continuing drop in salaried medical illustrator opportunities in medical schools and hospitals can make it more challenging to find work within an institution.

Perks

Anyone who loves art and biological science can find a rich outlet for their talents and interest in this field. The wide variety

Birck Cox, medical illustrator

Young Birck Cox was always a natural with pen and paper; in fact, he was still a kid growing up in southwest Washington State when his mom noticed that he could draw a picture of the family cat—with all its joints in the right place! In spite of that early interest in anatomical correctness, he graduated as an English major from Reed College in Portland, Oregon.

But after graduation, Cox discovered there were very few job opportunities for specialists in eighth-century Anglo-Saxon lyric verse, so he decided to support himself as a bicycle mechanic. Still, he knew he hadn't quite found his niche in life. "I knew that being a bike mechanic wasn't interesting enough to keep me going for the rest of my life," he says today. "I had passed my entire life knowing I could draw; I took art courses while in high school, but I didn't do it when I was in college. It was some kind of adolescent rebellion."

Eventually, he gave in to the lure of the paintbrush, and went back to school to study art and biology at Portland State University, ultimately earning an M.S. in medical illustration from the Medical College of Georgia in 1977.

After stints as resident medical illustrator at Texas Tech in Lubbock, the Medical College of Virginia at Richmond, and at the Penn State Hershey Medical Center, he went out on his own as a full-time freelancer in Philadelphia in 1994.

He's never looked back. As a freelancer, he's completed line art and wash for medical textbooks and journals; tone, color, and computer art for journals and advertising; and medical storyboards for a 3D-animation house. He's also coauthored a book on lower-limb amputation, currently draws a monthly column for a nursing magazine, and consults on an anesthesia journal for W.B. Saunders. He's even branched out into providing art for courtroom use. "Medical illustration for a court case can be decisive," he says. "In some cases, it's an important part of settling the case. That's one of the great advantages to using a medical illustrator. If it's done right, it can get the case to settle before it goes to court, which is often better for everyone."

He's amused when people wonder whether the need for medical illustrators might some day soon be evaporating. "What keeps the need for medical illustration current is that medicine is

(continues)

(continued)

changing constantly," he says. "If you look at any news show, there's going to be something about some advance in medicine." The idea of improvement or progress in medicine is part of the discipline, he notes, and as long as that's the case, there will be something for a medical illustrator to do. "I suppose you could use photography to take pictures of the anatomy, the rib cage, heart, lungs," he says. "It's all there in books, it's all been done before. But a doctor doesn't come to you to say: 'I need an illustration of a rib cage.' What he comes and asks is: 'I need a picture that shows the difference between a hole in the heart and blue baby syndrome, and I need it by Friday.'"

If you're interested in medical illustration, Cox warns that "there's a lot of blood and guts involved. One way or another, you're going to see guts." He also points out that there aren't very many programs to learn the field. "At one level, you could say that many are called, but few are chosen," he says. Another limiting factor for many artists is the scientific requirement. To get a master's in medical illustration requires a host of science courses, including anatomy, histology, pathology, neuroanatomy, and—in most cases—surgery. "I've known a lot of good artists," he says, "but they weren't ready for all the science. I did have a lingering affinity for biology, so I didn't feel out of my depth when I had to take science courses.

Interestingly, he doesn't spend much time creating art for his own pleasure, on his own time. If he does produce nonmedical art, it's typically done as a kind of drill, although he notes that this could be a peculiarity of his. "I did take an oil painting class a year ago. The teacher had an approach in mind I'd never dealt with." He's also a woodworker, and has built all the furniture in his studio.

One of his favorite parts of being a medical artist is offering a unique point of view. "I like being able to come up with a solution to the problem that the illustration presents that nobody has every seen before or thought of," he says. "It's presenting information in such a way that it does a better job of explaining something than everything I've ever seen before. "

---

of projects makes this career one of continuing and varied interest.

Get a Jump on the Job

You've got to be good at art and science to be a medical illustrator, so you can start early by drawing from life as much as possible. Take as many art and biological science courses as you can in high school. In college, concentrate on art (drawing, life drawing, painting, color theory, graphic design, illustration, and computer graphics) and science (general biology or zoology, vertebrate anatomy, developmental biology, chemistry, and cell biology). You should also take medical science courses, including human gross anatomy, pathology, histology/microanatomy, physiology, embryology, and neuroanatomy. In addition, most programs require an original master's thesis paper or a formal portfolio review for graduation.

MENTAL HEALTH ADVOCATE

OVERVIEW

A mental health advocate serves the community by helping people who suffer from mental illnesses get the help and services they need. The advocate might work for a private agency, a local or county agency, or for a state or federal organization, and may have children, adults, or both as clients. In any case, the problems related to mental illness can be quite varied, causing symptoms ranging anywhere from mildly annoying to completely debilitating.

Government statistics indicate that one in five Americans deals with some form of mental illness during the course of a year, and that nearly every family in America is affected at one time or another by mental illness. In addition, the rate at which people are being diagnosed with mental disorders is increasing. While people with a comfortable lifestyle and a support system of family or friends can usually obtain the mental health services they need, these days it can be more and more difficult. Many insurance plans don't pay for mental health care, and those that do often severely limit coverage. Disenfranchised people suffering from mental illness often find themselves adrift, with no one to speak for them.

A mental health advocate is available to help anyone who needs to get mental health care and is having trouble accessing services. The advocate can help the person

AT A GLANCE

Salary Range

The average salary for a mental health advocate ranges between $38,560 and $66,970. Directors of mental health agencies will earn more than other employees, and wages vary depending on how the agency is funded.

Education/Experience

You'll need at least a bachelor's degree, and probably a master's degree in an area such as psychology or social work. Some mental health advocates are licensed psychologists who have earned either master's or doctorate degrees.

Personal Attributes

Working with people who are mentally ill requires a great deal of patience and perseverance. Mentally ill people do not always act as you would expect them to, so it is important to be aware of your surroundings and what is occurring around you. You should be sensitive to people with problems, and able to work effectively within the mental health, law enforcement, and other systems to assure that your clients receive the help and services that they need.

Requirements

Requirements will vary. Some states require that mental health workers be licensed, while others require licensing only for those at certain levels of employment. You'll probably need to undergo background checks and, depending on your employer, possibly drug testing, as well.

Outlook

Jobs in the mental health field are expected to increase between 21 and 35 percent—a rate that is higher than average—through 2012. This is occurring because of increased demand for services. Many of these jobs, however, will require at least a master's degree.

Joe Conway, mental health advocate

Joe Conway has been working in the field of mental health for nearly 40 years, most of them with youth. These days, he's the director of an agency in Berks County, Pennsylvania, that provides advocacy services for children and adults. Most of the agency's funding comes from the United Way, and Conway is always looking for ways to supplement its budget. There is rarely enough money to do the work he'd like to do. "We're always the proverbial crisis clinic waiting to be washed over the waterfall," Conway says.

While financial support is one issue Conway grapples with, getting his services to the people who need them most is another. People suffering from mental illness aren't always capable of finding and accessing the help that they need. Conway and others within his agency work hard to assure that people who require assistance can find their way to help.

"Our agency is open to anyone who needs help," Conway says. "If someone calls us, we'll be there. Basically, our job is to help people stick up for their rights and their family's right. Our challenge is to be aware of everyone who needs us."

While there is no typical day for Conway, he usually spends some time each day dealing with paperwork, making phone calls to check up on clients or strategize with people from other support agencies, and working on ways to increase public awareness of his agency's work.

His work for clients varies greatly. He might work on getting someone into, or out of, a mental health hospital. He might work to have a child removed from an abusive home, help a pregnant teenager get the medical care she needs, arrange for school services for an autistic child, or help a client locate some temporary housing.

"I never know what the day will bring, but that certainly makes my job interesting," Conway says.

Conway's interest in mental health began early in his life. "My sister is mentally retarded—today they'd say developmentally delayed," he says. "I think my interest in this kind of work started from watching her difficulties and all the problems she had negotiating school and the community."

Conway, who has an undergraduate degree in special education and a master's degree in clinical psychology, says he sees an increasing need for mental health services in our communities. He attributes the need to many factors, including fear of what the future may hold, drugs, and economic pressures. People are incurring increasing levels of debt, and that is extremely stressful, he says. Parents are working longer and longer hours, leaving kids alone or unsupervised.

"The family is much more fragmented than it was in the 1960s," Conway says. "There's not as much attention available for kids, and that takes a heavy toll. We've created this nightmare for ourselves as a society."

Still, Conway enjoys his work. It can be extremely frustrating, and there always are concerns about funding and other issues. He tries, however, to focus on the good he is doing. "I try to focus on the successes," Conway says. "You can't help everyone, but you do what you can. You impact where you can, and hope for the best. You just do what you do—one person at a time."

navigate through red tape to make sure the mentally ill person is treated fairly. Depending on the situation, the advocate may intervene with law enforcement agencies, hospitals, social workers, schools, or community services on behalf of the client. Mental health advocates may even be asked to serve as a medical care agent for a person who is mentally ill and has no family. Advocates might also find themselves involved with issues such as eviction, working to obtain financial or other types of assistance, legal matters, and so forth.

Advocating for the mentally ill is not an easy job. Because mentally ill people may not always act rationally, they may be resistant to getting the help they need. They may want to be left alone or try to refuse the advocate's help. Some mental health advocates have even felt in danger while trying to help clients.

Mental health workers who advocate for children often work within schools to make sure children get the help they need. Some children with mental or emotional disorders qualify for full-time aides to stay with them during school hours.

Pitfalls

Advocating for someone who is mentally ill can be frustrating, because mental illness can be baffling, unpredictable, and draining. You may get very little response or appreciation from your clients for whom you work so hard—indeed, sometimes your clients may actually turn against you. You could work hard to get a client stabilized and back on track, only to find out in a day or two that he or she has had to return to the hospital or is in trouble with law enforcement. The job requires a great deal of documentation and paperwork, and although the work is extremely important, it doesn't typically pay as much as you'd earn working in a clinical setting.

Perks

It can be enormously satisfying to help those who cannot help themselves—one person at a time. You're likely to be surrounded by other people who care about making a difference in their communities.

Get a Jump on the Job

Volunteer to help in a nursing home, child day care, hospital, or anywhere else you'll be around people who need your help. This helps you to develop a level of empathy and understanding for people who may not be able to help themselves. Work on your empathetic listening skills, so you can really hear when people talk to you. Good communication skills are essential to being an effective advocate. Read books that describe mental disorders, especially looking for first-person or family accounts of the illnesses. This will help you to understand the range of mental illness and what it's like to experience a mental disorder.

MIDWIFE

OVERVIEW

While the term conjures up medieval health care during dark and uneducated times, midwives have been delivering babies for centuries. Today's modern midwives are as up-to-date as any other health care professional. Traditionally, midwives have been women, although some men in modern times have entered the field.

Generally, midwives attend to births that are uncomplicated and proceed as expected, and call on obstetricians or other doctors if the birth becomes more difficult. A midwife's first responsibility is to protect the well-being of both the mother and the unborn child. If there is any doubt, a doctor should be called or the mother moved to a medical facility as soon as possible. Although many midwives deliver babies at a client's home, others work in hospitals or doctors' offices as medical assistants, or in birthing centers or medical clinics. Some larger obstetrics practices also keep at least one midwife on staff for those women who prefer midwife care.

The traditional midwife philosophy states that birth is a natural process that should get as little interference as is safe and possible. Midwives generally advocate natural childbirth and birth education, and sometimes use alternative birthing methods such as underwater birth. Most consider a birth to be a family affair, including not only Mom and Dad, but siblings, grandparents, and any other interested parties.

All midwives must pass an exam in order to be certified, and certified midwives must follow the same professional standards and ethics as a nurse-midwife.

AT A GLANCE

Salary Range

The average salary for a certified nurse-midwife is about $79,000. A certified midwife who is not also a nurse usually earns less than a certified nurse-midwife. Salary can vary greatly depending on location and other factors.

Education/Experience

Educational requirements vary depending on whether you want to be a certified midwife or a certified nurse-midwife. To be a certified midwife, you'll need at least a four-year college degree, but you won't need to be licensed as a registered nurse, which requires additional schooling. A certified nurse-midwife must have completed an accredited nursing program and be licensed as a registered nurse.

Personal Attributes

You should be able to relate well to patients, and be compassionate and genuinely concerned with creating an optimal childbirth experience. Also, you must have the ability to think and act quickly and logically when under pressure. You should be in good physical condition and have good stamina, as childbirth sometimes takes a long time.

Requirements

Requirements vary from state to state, but midwifery is nationally regulated. All midwives, whether or not they are nurses, must be certified.

Outlook

Favorable. The number of women using midwives has increased during the past several years, and is expected to continue to do so. However, the demand for midwives varies depending on location and whether the area is rural or urban as well as other factors.

Midwives share a commitment to women's health care.

A certified midwife, sometimes called a direct-entry midwife, enters the field without having formal nursing education. She may complete an apprenticeship or be trained in a community-based program.

A certified nurse-midwife, who is licensed as a registered nurse in addition to having earned midwife certification, often collaborates with doctors and works with other medical professionals to provide a full range of services to her client. Most nurse-midwives and certified midwives provide some level of follow-up care for patients, and offer education on breast-feeding, postpartum care, emotional issues that sometimes follow childbirth, child care, and other issues.

As with most other aspects of medical care, midwifery has become more complicated as insurance providers have gotten involved and regulations have grown. In some areas, however, midwives still deal directly with patients for payment, and, in some cases, may even exchange services in lieu of payment.

Midwifery is an ancient profession involving a powerful partnership between a woman in labor and a trained expert in

Donna Knox, midwife

Donna Knox of Verbena, Alabama, calls herself a traditional midwife. She learned midwifery by attending training classes and conferences over a period of years, until she had accumulated enough knowledge to pass the certification exam. The owner of MorningStar Birth Services, she has four assistants who work with her in attending home births.

The best thing about being a midwife, she says, is experiencing the strength of the woman giving birth. "I also enjoy educating women that birth is a normal procedure, not a medical one, and is best done at home," she says.

When Knox gets a call that one of her clients has a baby on the way, she decides whether to head over and see what's going on, or to wait until the contractions are closer together and stronger. She believes it's important for expectant parents to have some time and space to themselves in the early stages of labor. "They have to learn to enact the birth dance together," she says.

When she and her assistant do arrive at the home, they assess the mother-to-be and determine her physical and emotional needs. Fulfilling those needs might be the job of family members or other caregivers, or Knox might take care of them herself. It is very important, she says, to offer emotional support that keeps the mother centered as the birth becomes more imminent. As the baby gets closer to being born, Knox, who has been working as a midwife for six years, stays closer to the mother, anticipating any needs, possible problems, or other issues.

Knox says the work is physically, mentally, and emotionally draining, but that she can't imagine any other work that's more rewarding. She enjoys working with women and their families, and seeing families expand as new babies are born.

She assists with water births when requested, and also provides nutritional counseling, information about herbal products, and other services.

"What I like best about my work is helping women find their strength and power," she says, "and seeing a woman change as she gives birth into a very strong person who can face any situation in life."

birthing. During the birth, the midwife supports a woman in a natural but very intense and potentially frightening experience. It's extremely important for a midwife to have an excellent reputation for being thorough, professional, and kind. Midwives must practice excellent sanitation practices and adhere to all professional standards.

Pitfalls

A midwife never works "regular hours," and often may find it difficult to make plans because of the unpredictability of childbirth. She must often be on call for patients who are nearing their due dates. Delivering babies is hard work, and, although most midwives find it to be incredibly rewarding, it can be emotionally draining. In the event that something goes wrong during the birth, it can be extremely stressful, and even, in rare cases, cause for great grief. While midwifery is becoming increasingly accepted, there are still people who look at midwives with suspicion and consider them to be less qualified than doctors to deliver babies.

Perks

Most midwives love their work and find it to be extremely rewarding. Many midwives consider their work to be a calling—not just a job. The miracle of birth is a joy to witness, and midwives get to go a step beyond witnessing—they assist.

Get a Jump on the Job

Learn all that you can about childbirth and midwifery. There are some excellent documentaries about childbirth available, and numerous books and articles. If you know someone well who is expecting a baby, consider asking if you might observe the birth, particularly if the delivery is to be done at home. Or, if you know a midwife, you could ask if you could accompany her to births, assuming that the family would not object to your presence. If you have the opportunity, talk to a midwife about her job and what it's like. You can find some midwife directories on line, and some midwives have their own Web sites, where you may be able to locate some advice and information about the career.

MUSEUM DISPLAY DESIGNER

OVERVIEW

A collection of artifacts, regardless of how valuable or rare, is just a pile of stuff if it's stacked up and covered with dust in an attic someplace. Once someone (usually a museum curator) locates and obtains those artifacts, they can be cleaned, restored, and displayed for all to see, enjoy, and learn from.

Basically, it's the job of a museum display designer to decide how to most effectively and attractively display each piece of an exhibit, while assuring the safety of each item.

The exhibits must convey information, while attracting enough attention to draw people to the display. The designer also ensures the objects remain safe while on display. He or she must consider lighting, dust, crowd control, and many other factors that could affect the items on exhibit. Other objects, such as gems, leather items, books, and glass, all have special requirements for storage, handling, and display.

The duties of a museum display designer vary. Generally, you'll work with the curator to decide how items would be best presented. Display cases, cabinets, risers, stands, shelves, and mounts may be used to exhibit items, and may have to be built to specification. As a museum display designer, you'll need to work with Plexiglas, fabric, wood, and other materials.

AT A GLANCE

Salary Range

The average salary for a museum display designer is $30,000 but salaries vary tremendously, depending on the type, size, and location of the museum and other factors.

Education/Experience

Bachelor's degree in archaeology or anthropology. Some museum display designers have an art background, or have graduated from a design school. If you're planning to work in an art museum, an art background with a concentration in art history would be useful.

Personal Attributes

You should be able to communicate effectively with others about design concepts and ideas, and to think abstractly, with good visualization skills. You should have steady nerves and be able to work under deadline pressure—displays must sometimes be built quickly to accommodate museum scheduling. You should be creative, yet thorough and detail oriented about keeping track of supplies and artifacts. And you must be able to make sound decisions and judgments when problems arise.

Requirements

Because you'll probably be handling valuable pieces of art and other objects, many museums will require a background check. And because the physical work involved with the job can be considerable, some employers will ask that you undergo a preemployment physical. Drug screening may also be required.

Outlook

Jobs as museum display designers are expected to increase at about an average rate through 2012, according to government statistics. That means job growth will be between 10 and 20 percent.

A museum display designer also needs to know about packaging and packing items for transport from the museum, and unpacking items coming into the museum. After all, you can't just throw a 2,000-year-old ritual mask into a box and hope it

Rolland Hower, museum display designer

When Rolland Hower was the chief of natural history exhibits for the Smithsonian Institution in Washington, D.C., one of his jobs was to design a display for the famous Hope diamond. The idea, Hower says, was to figure out how to show off the diamond to its very best advantage, while assuring that it would remain safe and secure while being viewed by thousands.

To do that, he designed a safe made of metal and bulletproof glass that could be opened for viewing purposes and then sealed when the museum's doors closed each night. The Hope Diamond exhibit, which is part of the gem hall that Hower designed for the Smithsonian, was anchored in concrete to ensure that the safe wouldn't be picked up and carted off. "The safe was literally poured into a concrete base," Hower recalls.

These days, however, Hower's design work is a little more laid back and a lot less stressful. He currently serves as the principal designer of exhibits at the Grandfather Mountain Nature Museum, located in the Blue Ridge Mountains in North Carolina. Hower designed a gem and mineral hall for the museum on Grandfather Mountain, which focuses on the natural history of the region in which it's located. While designing the gem and mineral display, he worked with an expert gemologist who guided him on the best stones and gems to display, and how each stone should be treated.

"I can't know everything about every stone, so I have to depend on an expert for help," Hower says. He also depends on a local craftsman to create models of much of the plant life on Grandfather Mountain, using wax and other materials to recreate the local fauna and flora.

In the past years, Hower has increasingly depended on computer programs to help him design displays. With the aid of the computer, he recently designed a 56 x 5 foot wall, portraying all the animals found on Grandfather Mountain. The computer program, he explains, helped him figure out where and how to best place each animal on the wall.

Hower stumbled onto this job by a circuitous route. He started out as a commercial artist, who then decided to get an engineering degree. Once he'd done that, he followed his interest in science and earned a Ph.D. in biology. "Sometimes it takes a while to figure out what you want to do," Hower explains. If you're thinking about a career in museum display design, Hower suggests you go first to art school but focus on an area that you find particularly interesting, such as science or history. This kind of educational preparation will help because designing a museum display requires both the ability to present material in an attractive, eye-catching manner, and understanding the materials with which you're working.

Hower has managed to combine his love of art and science in his job at Grandfather Mountain, which is a widely recognized nature preserve and home of the Mile-High Swinging Bridge. "The idea," he explains, "is to be able to present information in an attractive, yet intelligent manner. Exhibit people just describe the way things are."

survives the trip, or use a wedge and hammer to break open a box containing priceless gemstones.

Consider for a moment the great variety of items that are exhibited in museums. In addition to great artwork, you can go to a museum to see antique aircraft, often suspended from the museum ceiling. There are historical museums that reenact scenes or events with life-size figures and objects, all carefully arranged for the best viewing. You might see collections of photographs, greeting cards, or postcards; a preserved and mounted Grizzly bear; an Egyptian mummy; a collection of Civil War or World War II uniforms; or a collection of rare seashells or gemstones. There are many types of museums, and millions of displays of objects of nearly every sort.

For that reason, a museum display designer must be extremely creative and able to think outside the box. You wouldn't, after all, display an exhibit of old blacksmithing equipment the same way you'd display the Hope diamond. A collection of Louis XIV French antique furniture most likely would be exhibited differently from a butterfly collection. Every exhibit must be carefully evaluated and assessed, and then a decision made on the best way to show it off.

Pitfalls

The work of a museum display designer can be tedious, depending on the type of exhibit and number of items involved. Handling extremely valuable objects can cause some stress. Also, museum display designer jobs tend to be competitive; once you've landed a job, you'll need to keep up with the latest trends and innovations.

Perks

Every time the museum gets a new display, you not only get a new job opportunity, but you get insight into what you may find to be a whole new world. You'll get the first look at every display that comes into the museum, and get to know each item well as you determine how to best exhibit it. You'll have the opportunity to use your creative skills, and in some cases, you'll get to make history come alive for museum visitors.

Get a Jump on the Job

There are various paths you can take if you wish to be a museum designer. If you're absolutely fascinated with natural history, for instance, start learning all you can about minerals, plants, animals, and natural phenomena. Take some art courses, and start learning about design, lighting, fabric, 2-D and 3-D art, colors, and spacing.

PALLIATIVE CARE PROFESSIONAL

OVERVIEW

A cross between a health care worker and a hospice worker, palliative care professionals work with terminally ill patients to ease symptoms, but they don't cure the underlying disease. For the last 30 years, palliative care has been provided by hospice programs for dying Americans. Currently these programs serve more than one million patients and their families each year. Today, this same approach to care—now called "palliative care"—is being used by other health care providers, including teams in hospitals, nursing facilities, and home health agencies in combination with other medical treatments to help people who are seriously ill. Palliative care professionals often work as part of a team including physicians, nurses, social workers, chaplains, volunteers, and home health aides. Each provides assistance based on his or her own area of expertise.

To "palliate" means to make comfortable by treating a person's symptoms from an illness. Hospice and palliative care both focus on helping a person be comfortable by addressing the problems that are causing physical or emotional pain or suffering. Hospice and other palliative care providers have teams of people working together to improve the quality of a seriously ill person's life and to support that person and their family during and after treatment.

There are some important differences between hospice care and palliative care.

AT A GLANCE

Salary Range

Salary ranges enormously depending on whether the professional is a doctor, registered nurse, nurse practitioner, social worker, or licensed practical nurse.

Education/Experience

Varies depending on what type of palliative care professional—almost always includes college, with either a nursing degree of some type, a social work degree, or an M.D. A variety of universities, colleges, professional organizations, and online courses offer palliative care training programs for health care professionals.

Personal Attributes

Sensitivity, excellent communication skills, interest in others and in health care, ability to handle end-of-life issues with dignity and grace.

Requirements

Some colleges offer a certificate in palliative care. The National Board for Certification of Hospice and Palliative Nurses (NBCHPN) also certifies qualified hospice and palliative nurses. Once certified, the advanced practice nurse, registered nurse, licensed practical/vocational nurse or nursing assistant is entitled to use the appropriate credentials: APRN, BC-PCM (advanced practice registered nurse, Board Certified-Palliative Care Management); CHPN (certified hospice and palliative nurse); CHPLN (certified hospice and palliative licensed nurse); or CHPNA (certified hospice and palliative nursing assistant).

Outlook

Excellent. As the population ages, there will be an increased need for trained, compassionate palliative care professionals in hospices, nursing homes, and hospitals.

While hospice focuses on easing symptoms and supporting patients with a life expectancy of a few months, palliative care may be given at any time during a patient's illness—even right after the diagnosis. Anyone with a serious illness, regardless of life expectancy, can receive palliative care

Most hospices have a set of defined services, team members, and rules and regulations. Some hospices provide palliative care as a separate program or service, which can be very confusing to patients and families. You may receive palliative care and curative care at the same time, but with hospice, only treatments aimed at relieving symptoms are provided.

In addition to medical training (many palliative care professionals are nurses), palliative professionals must be prepared

to handle the legal, psychological, and ethical issues associated with death. A palliative care professional can help the patient and family identify what the goals of care should be based on their needs, wants, and desires, and then help the patient and family create a plan of care based on those goals.

Palliative care tries to relieve the suffering and enhance the quality of life in people living with acute or chronic life-threatening illnesses, as well as during their death and in the bereavement process. A palliative care professional therefore pays attention to a patient's physical, psychosocial, and spiritual concerns as the end

Nathan Goldstein, M.D., palliative care professional

When he started out in his medical training, Nathan Goldstein knew he wanted to be a doctor. But after finishing an elective in palliative care during his medical residency at Mount Sinai Medical Center in New York City, he suddenly realized exactly how he wanted to spend the rest of his career. "For the first time I was being encouraged to sit down by the bedside of a patient and really try to figure out what was going on with them," he says, "to get to know them in a very profound, intimate way at what was such a pivotal point in all of their lives. I thought: 'This is it! This is exactly why I went into medicine!'

"It is a privilege to be involved with patients and their families at this point in their lives, to share in this experience. As awful as this experience may be for them, it's a privilege to try to relieve their suffering, physically and emotionally. It is," he says simply, "a gift."

Now assistant professor of geriatrics and medicine at Mount Sinai School of Medicine, Dr. Goldstein sees patients on the inpatient palliative care consult service. He teaches at all levels—medical students, residents, fellows—and also does research in the field. But an important part of his job is interacting with patients. "We see all kinds of patients at all points of disease," he says. "We'll see patients very early in the course of cancer, with moderately to severe heart failure, lung disease. We see patients with dementia who are actively dying, and we're called in and they pass away. Some are young, some are older, some are very early in their disease with no symptoms at all but who need emotional support. We like to get to know them early. Sometimes, we have patients at the other end of the spectrum who can't talk to us but whose family need lots of emotional support in terms of a loved one dying. We focus at all points across the whole spectrum."

(continues)

(continued)

Dealing every day with patients who are critically ill and dying seems to a lot of people like sad, depressing work, but Dr. Goldstein sees it differently. "Sometimes the work is sad," he says, "because a lot of our patients do die. But the way I think of it, my job is to relieve suffering—not only for the patient, but also for the family. When a patient dies, the family lives on for 30, 40, or 50 years afterwards. We need to make sure the patient's death is as comfortable as it can be for the patient, as well as for their family, because they will continue to remember. It's really uplifting to feel like I do good both in the moment, and in the future."

Like any job, there are pluses and minuses, Dr. Goldstein says. "I think like any professional we're busy, we work long, hard hours. But the trade-off is so great! I may be exhausted when I do go home, but I know I've done really great work that day."

If you're interested in the health field, the palliative care field is growing and becoming much better known. "This is the time to get involved," he says. "Learn as much as you can, whenever you have the opportunity. If you get the chance to volunteer or do an elective or rotation in palliative care, whether it be as a high school student, a medical student, a nursing student—seek out opportunities. Unfortunately, palliative care options are not found in every hospital. But just because it's not in the same building or around the corner, don't give up. It may take a little bit of work to find a place to train, but the work is so rewarding, you won't be sorry."

of life nears. Many of these professionals work in hospices, but others work in hospitals and nursing homes.

Pitfalls

It can be a difficult and sobering job to deal only with patients who are not going to get better. Even the most insightful and sensitive souls can eventually become overburdened with the endless grieving inherent in this job.

Perks

While this can be a difficult area of health care, this career can offer an incredibly rewarding gift of helping those at the end of their lives pass on with dignity and peace. As people age and need palliative care, a new respect for this specialty is emerging.

Get a Jump on the Job

This is most likely a challenging profession for young people to consider. Volunteering at your church or synagogue or at a nursing home or hospital is probably the best place to start. How do you feel about working with critically ill patients? Do you feel comfortable in the health care scene? These are questions to ask yourself as you begin to volunteer. Consider health care internships and read widely in the field of death and dying. Think about which area of palliative care you're interested in—as a nurse, physician, counselor, or social worker—and take the appropriate courses.

PARASITOLOGIST

OVERVIEW

There's a whole world out there you never see, teeming with life—the world of viruses, bacteria, worms, insects, and an incredible number of other parasites that use people, animals, and plants as their hosts. Parasitologists are the scientists who study these creatures, and the effects they have on their hosts and the environment.

There are as many different areas of parasitology as there are parasitologists to work in them, including the agricultural and aquacultural industries, diagnostic laboratories, the veterinary field, hospitals, food and beverage companies, biotechnology firms, pharmaceutical companies, and industrial labs. While much of their work is conducted in laboratories, parasitologists often venture out into the field to check for or collect parasites, or to observe their effects.

The reason there are so many areas of parasitology is that parasites affect the world in so many different ways. There actually are a greater number of species of parasites than of free-living species, which is unfortunate, since parasites cause disease in humans. For example, parasitic diseases such as malaria cause more than one million deaths each year in developing nations. Parasitic tapeworms, blood flukes, and hookworms can be lethal, and insect parasites such as fleas and ticks also can spread diseases such as bubonic plague and typhus. Scientists who study parasites in connection with human disease are called medical parasitologists.

Parasites also cause disease in animals, which can indirectly affect human health. Farm crops, farm-raised fish, and animals raised for food all are subject to parasitic diseases, which can affect both our food supply and our health. Agriculture parasitologists work with parasites in connection with crops; aquaculture parasitologists work with fish, and veterinary parasitologists work with animals. Wildlife and fishery parasitologists study the effects of parasites on wild animals and fish populations, usually working for government agencies or universities. They survey wild animals and fish for disease and work to reduce the effects of the parasites.

Other parasitologists study the biochemistry and molecular biology of parasites. Some work to develop vaccines against parasites, or work in ecological

Dr. Susan Bower, parasitologist

The shadowy world of shellfish parasites may be an unlikely place to start a career, but for parasitologist Susan Bower, that makes it all the more interesting. Because not much scientific research has been conducted on shellfish, most of the parasites she sees have never been seen before. "There's not much known about the diseases of shellfish," she says. "Because of that, most of the parasites we encounter are brand new to science. That keeps my work very interesting and exciting."

It is that unknown quality of parasitology, in fact, that makes it such a rewarding career for Bower. "What appeals to me is the element of the unknown, and trying to understand the way it all works," she says.

Because there is a lot of interest in culturing shellfish, it's important to know what sorts of parasites they attract and how the shellfish and their environments are affected by parasites.

Bower is employed by the Canadian government and heads the Shellfish Diseases Research Program in British Columbia, works with local shellfish harvesters, who often alert her to changes in shellfish or their environments. "If they see something that they haven't seen before they'll tell me, and I'll go out and do some field sampling. Often, I find that diseases in shellfish are caused by parasites," Bower says.

Because there has been relatively little research to date on diseases of shellfish, Bower and some of her colleagues are writing a comprehensive description of their findings. She also is working to establish regulations that would protect the health of shellfish.

While she enjoys being out in the field, administrative work takes up most of her time these days, but she's philosophical about the need for documentation. "There's no point in conducting the research if you're not going to write and publish the results," Bower says. "And, there are manuals and other works that need to be written and put together. It's all part of the job, and it's all important."

Her work has taken Bower to Brazil, Korea, Spain, Portugal, China, and Thailand, where she conducts research and meets with colleagues. Bower was always interested in biology, but says she finds parasites to be particularly fascinating. "There are so many sorts of parasites and so much more we can learn about them," Bower says. "Parasites affect everyone, and it's important that we know all that we can about them."

parasitology. Still others teach parasitology at colleges and universities.

Pitfalls

It takes a significant amount of education to become a parasitologist, which involves considerable time and expense. Without a Ph.D., you may have trouble finding a job, although you may be able to work in a related field, such as biology. Project deadlines can be stressful, sometimes requiring many long work days.

Perks

Parasitologists are on the cutting edge of many scientific endeavors, and play an important role in solving problems that affect people all around the world. Parasitologists often enter the field because they have a great interest in helping to improve conditions, are generally committed to their work, and find it to be rewarding, challenging, and enjoyable.

Get a Jump on the Job

Take as many science courses—particularly biology and related sciences—as you can, and learn everything possible about parasites. There are many books available about parasites, some of which are suggested in the appendix in the back of this book.

PERFUSIONIST

OVERVIEW

Clinical perfusionists quite literally hold life in their hands. But what exactly do they do?

It's a fancy name, but basically "perfusion" means "the passage of fluid through tissue." A perfusionist is a health care specialist who uses a number of highly technical, mechanical, and electronic devices to make sure that oxygen moves throughout a patient's body via the blood, even when the patient's lungs and heart aren't functioning.

It's the perfusionist who controls the heart-lung machine that temporarily takes over a patient's breathing and blood circulation during open-heart surgery. During many types of open-heart surgery, the patient's heart must be stopped so that the surgeon can work on it. To do this, the patient's blood is diverted away from the heart and lungs into a heart-lung machine. The heart-lung machine removes the blood from the body, oxygenates it, and then returns the blood to the patient. A perfusionist is responsible for operating the machine during surgery, monitoring the circulatory process, taking appropriate corrective action when a problem crops up, and keeping both the surgeon and the anesthesiologist informed as to the patient's condition.

In addition to the operation of the heart-lung machine during surgery, perfusionists often function in supportive roles for other medical specialties in operating mechanical devices to assist in the conservation of blood and blood products during surgery, and provide extended, long-term

AT A GLANCE

Salary Range

Median annual earnings of certified clinical perfusionists are about $65,000, with a low of $45,000 and a high of $80,000.

Education/Experience

A college degree is required by many perfusion schools, although some do not. Biology, chemistry, and physics are a requirement for most programs. Some programs also require organic chemistry and a year of calculus. Check the individual schools for more specifics. Most perfusion programs are two years long; some are degree programs and some aren't. When it comes to getting a job as a perfusionist the only thing that matters is being certified, which you will be upon finishing a perfusion program. There are at least 15 perfusionist schools in the country, each associated with a hospital.

Personal Attributes

Ability to handle stress, calmness under pressure, interest in medicine, attention to detail.

Requirements

Perfusionists must be certified, and in some states a license is also required.

Outlook

Job openings for perfusionists (also called circulation technologists) in the United States are increasing due to the growing number of people age 65 and older who are more likely to develop cardiovascular disease and require open heart surgery. In addition, new procedures for many types of heart disease, defects, and disorders are increasing the need for cardiovascular perfusion services. Employment of perfusionists may grow faster than the average for all occupations through the year 2010 as the volume of cardiac surgery increases, according to the Bureau of Labor Statistics. The number of surgical procedures is also expected to rise as the population grows and ages.

support of the patient's circulation outside of the operating room environment. The exact duties and responsibilities of a perfusionist are often dependent upon the particular institution where an individual works.

During surgery, perfusionists also routinely administer various types of blood products and medications, and control the temperature of patients. Together with doctors, perfusionists also are responsible for selecting the most appropriate equipment and techniques during surgery. As well as operating the heart-lung machine, perfusionists also monitor, test, and control a range of patient indicators, such as arterial and venous blood gas status, kidney function, clotting and fluid balance, acid/base status, temperature, and heart cell protection.

But that's not all. Perfusionists may also perform administrative duties, such as purchasing equipment and supplies, hiring support technicians, department management, and quality improvement. They must handle very stressful situations, pay close attention to detail and stay abreast of new developments in their profession.

You'll find a perfusionist in the surgical suite of a variety of operations,

Dan Downing, chief perfusionist

The son and grandson of physicians, it's not too surprising that Dan Downing headed down the health care path after graduation from college (where he majored in the arts).

"It turns out that, as it happens, my father was a pediatric cardiologist," Downing recalls, "and his best friend was a cardiac surgeon." When his mother and the surgeon's wife were having lunch one day, Downing was talking to the women about his future plans. "The surgeon's wife asked me if I'd ever thought about running a heart-lung machine, and would I be interested in trying," Downing said. "I said, sure." At that point, he'd never seen a heart-lung machine. "I was envisioning an iron lung, which was as close as I could come in my mind to what they were talking about," he says. The next thing he knew, he was watching an open heart surgery at a local hospital with his dad. "I looked at the [heart-lung machine]—it was basically a machine, and it's a plumbing problem. 'I can do this,' I think. 'This is simple.'"

Downing became an apprentice perfusionist, since there were no schools that taught perfusion skills back then. As he made the rounds of Philadelphia hospitals, one day the person training to become a perfusionist at one of the hospitals didn't show up. "So I became the chief trainee," he recalls. Then one day at dinner, a surgeon he was training with had an emergency case and he couldn't find a perfusionist. "They were in trouble," Downing recalls. "The patient's aortic valve had torn lose. The doctor said: 'Can you do this?' I said: 'Is the patient going to die?' and he said 'Yes.' So I said: 'I can do this!' I rushed in and once you did it once, you went on the payroll. Today, there are schools that train perfusionists in two- to six-year programs, so that the student may end up with a master's degree, although there are also Ph.D.s in perfusion.

Downing is glad he got into the perfusionist business when he did, because "this job plays to a lot of my strengths: concentration, observation, great mechanical skills, and relatively good people skills. That's certainly helpful—you're working in an environment with nurses, technicians,

(continues)

(continued)

anesthesiologists, surgeons, administrators, orderlies, salesmen . . . a whole vast range of personalities and levels of input you have to deal with. If you're a shrinking violet, you're not going to last long with a cardiac surgeon. "

The hardest part of the job, Downing says, is the uncertainty. "It's something one has to live with," he says philosophically. At a minimum, he's on call 50 percent of the time, which is an improvement on the old days, when he was on call 24-7, except for two weeks when the surgeons went on vacation. "There is always uncertainty," he says. "Even in surgeries done off bypass [without a heart-lung machine], we're still there, right across the hall, and the heart-lung machine is primed. There is tremendous uncertainty." They wait for that emergency, he says, when the surgeon realizes: We have to go on bypass—*now*.

The hours are also hard to pin down. "You have no guarantee," he explains. "It can be one graft taking three hours, or it could take 10 hours. You just don't know. And you don't have the option of putting it in the drawer and working on it tomorrow. That's the worst part of it."

Still, he loves his job. "I've told my daughter, if you're really really lucky, you'll find something you love to do, that you're good at, and that you can make a living at." Admitting it's a stressful job, Downing says he actually likes the stress. "I need stress. Lots of people don't realize they need stress. People who are in stressful jobs are probably there for a reason. I'm one of them. I've also made a good living at it. Those have all been important things. I think it's a wonderful job, it's been a wonderful career for me," he says. "I've been able to do something which is important."

---

including coronary artery bypass surgery, heart valve replacement, heart lung transplantation, congenital heart defect repair, and artificial heart support. Perfusionists are also involved in other surgical areas such as orthopedics, oncology, and liver transplantation.

Pitfalls

This is a high-stress job that usually requires people to be on call 24 hours a day for weeks on end. Even in certain operations that do not require a heart-lung machine, perfusionists must stand by in case the situation calls for a sudden need for this machine. In addition, technological changes continue to raise the question of whether perfusionists will continue to be in demand in the future.

Perks

People in the health care field typically seek out this type of work because they want to help people, and this is certainly true for perfusionists. Helping to save lives is a significant reason why people enjoy this job.

Get a Jump on the Job

There's not much chance of helping out on a heart-lung machine while you're still in high school, but you can certainly volunteer in a hospital to see if you enjoy the atmosphere. Read widely in the fields of science, medicine, and health care, and take lots of science courses (especially chemistry and biology) in high school. Perfusion schools don't require a particular major, but biology, chemistry, or physics provide a good background for this area.

PHLEBOTOMIST

OVERVIEW

If you've ever donated blood or had a blood test, you've been on the receiving end of the services of a phlebotomist—a medical technician who draws blood for analysis, transfusions, donations, or research. You'll find phlebotomists in hospitals and clinics, doctor's offices, diagnostic medical laboratories, and nursing homes. Less traditional job locations for phlebotomists include weight loss centers, DUI clinics, health fairs, mobile blood donation facilities, public health facilities, nursing homes, drug rehabilitation centers, and veterinarian's offices.

While phlebotomists are professional health care workers, they don't require nearly the same level of training as do other professionals. Requirements vary from state to state and employer to employer, but most phlebotomy jobs require only six months to a year of part-time training. Still, it's important for phlebotomists to understand the circulatory system and have a sound knowledge of basic anatomy. Safety awareness also is extremely important for phlebotomists, who could be at risk of contracting serious diseases if they accidentally stick themselves with needles used on infected patients. Phlebotomists must be carefully trained in infection control and sterilization practices, and need to understand basic medical procedures.

Because phlebotomists work directly with patients, it's important to have a pleasant bedside manner, and to be able to reassure patients who don't like the idea

AT A GLANCE

Salary Range

The salary range for a phlebotomist is between $18,720 and $25,168, depending on experience, location, and the type of facility by which you're employed. The median salary is $22,000, according to numbers released by the American Society for Clinical Pathology.

Education/Experience

You'll need to have finished high school or earned a graduate equivalency degree. Most employers will require that you've completed coursework at a community college or technical school, but some will train on the job.

Personal Attributes

A phlebotomist should be patient and caring, because many people are uncomfortable with having blood taken. You need to be able to work carefully in order to adhere to safety regulations and to make sure the needle used to draw blood is in the proper spot. Obviously, you can't be a phlebotomist if you have an aversion to being around blood.

Requirements

Most employers will require that you be certified to work as a phlebotomist. Some states offer certification programs, as do some national organizations, such as the American Society for Clinical Pathology, American Medical Technologists, and the American Society for Phlebotomy Technicians. Once you're certified, you'll be recognized as a certified phlebotomy technician (CPT) or a registered phlebotomy technician (RPT). You must be recertified each year in order to maintain your status as a CPT or RPT.

Outlook

Jobs in phlebotomy are expected to increase at about an average rate of between 10 and 20 percent through 2012, according to government statistics.

Carol Conrad, phlebotomist

Carol Conrad was scared to death the first time she had to stick a needle in another person's arm during her training to become a phlebotomist. Eleven years later, she thinks nothing of taking blood from 30 to 35 people at once—and that's just on her morning rounds!

Conrad works the day shift in a busy hospital in Reading, Pennsylvania, along with seven to nine other phlebotomists. On a typical day, her team begins its shift by drawing blood from between 300 and 350 patients.

There are many reasons to check the blood of hospital patients. It's tested for all sorts of things, including blood sugar; heart, liver, or kidney enzymes; infections; blood consistency; and blood counts. And because blood can change often, it's important to check it often, Conrad says.

Conrad and the other phlebotomists on her team pick up pre-labeled vials listing the patient's name, room number, how many vials are needed, and other important information. A bar-coded identification system used at the hospital makes it easy to positively identify patients and to keep the blood sorted out and properly identified.

"There's no way you can stick the wrong person with this system," Conrad says. "But, before we had this system, you had to be very careful about keeping everything straight."

Blood is sent back to the lab as the phlebotomists progress through their rounds, allowing lab technicians to begin analyzing it. For the rest of the day, Conrad and other phlebotomists are available to draw blood from patients in their area who have orders to be retested, and to go to other parts of the hospital, when necessary. They also go off campus to participate in health fairs at businesses, industrial facilities, and other locations. "Anywhere there's a health fair offering a cholesterol check, you've got to have some phlebotomists," Conrad explains.

Conrad, who began nursing school but realized that wasn't the field for her, got into phlebotomy because she thought it would be interesting and because she likes being around people. She says it's important to be able to get along with patients, supervisors, coworkers, doctors, nurses, and other hospital staff.

"It helps if you like to talk to people," Conrad says. "Some patients are really nervous about having blood drawn, and some don't understand why it has to be done so often. You need sometimes to be able to take a few minutes to explain what you're doing and why it needs to be done. You have to build a little trust."

Conrad was trained on the job, and she advises anyone who wants to be a phlebotomist to get some training, and also to become certified. In her county, she says, the community college offers both six-month and nine-month courses for students working toward becoming phlebotomists. Most employers no longer hire people without training, she says.

Conrad very much enjoys working as a phlebotomist, and says she would recommend the job to someone interested in the medical profession. "I think that someone could start as a phlebotomist, get additional training or schooling, and work their way into another area of the profession," Conrad says. "It seems to be a good starting point. And it's an important job."

of needles. As you get more skilled and experienced, finding the right vein and the actual process of drawing blood becomes much easier. You'll gain confidence that will allow you to work more quickly and accurately.

Pitfalls

Phlebotomy is one of the lowest-paying jobs in the medical industry because it does not require extensive training. Some phlebotomists find that the work of drawing blood gets tedious and tiresome when it needs to be done continuously for long periods of time.

Perks

Phlebotomy is a good career for people who are interested in entering the medi-cal profession, but don't have the time, financial resources, or ability to spend on years of education and training. And you'll work closely with patients, which is an advantage if you're someone who enjoys frequent contact with others.

Get a Jump on the Job

You could begin checking to see if there is a community college or technical school in your area that offers courses and training in phlebotomy. Some hospitals also offer courses. Learn what you can about the circulatory system, basic anatomy, the properties of blood, and other topics that relate to phlebotomy.

PHYSICAL THERAPIST

OVERVIEW

Physical therapists work with patients who are recovering from or learning to live with physical disabilities resulting from accidents, illnesses, birth defects, or other infirmities. Physical therapists work to improve mobility and function in patients, restore use of limbs, and relieve pain. Often they're working to improve the quality of life for patients who are temporarily or permanently disabled from stroke, head trauma, or chronic back pain, arthritis, cerebral palsy, broken bones, or other conditions.

You'll find physical therapists in nursing homes, hospitals, rehabilitation hospitals, physicians' offices, schools, and private clinics. Some physical therapists are self-employed and contract with home healthcare agencies, adult day care programs, schools, hospitals, and rehabilitation facilities. Also, employers sometimes hire physical therapists to assess workplaces and make suggestions on how workers can do their jobs more safely. Other therapists teach in physical therapy programs and conduct research.

As a physical therapist, your first task after meeting a new patient is to evaluate the person to determine the exact problems. During the evaluation, you'll study the patient's medical history and perform a series of tests to determine the patient's mobility, strength, motor functions, balance, and coordination. You'll need to take a realistic look at the limitations of your patient to try to figure out how well

AT A GLANCE

Salary Range

The average salary for a physical therapist ranges between $48,480 and $70,050, according to government statistics. The highest 10 percent earn more than $86,260, while the lowest 10 percent earn less than $42,000.

Education/Experience

Education requirements for physical therapists are stringent—you'll need a bachelor's degree, and either a master's or doctorate degree from an accredited program. According to the Commission on Accreditation in Physical Therapy Education, the accreditation arm of the American Physical Therapy Association, all accredited physical therapy programs must offer master's degrees or higher. Your undergraduate degree should include courses in anatomy, physics, mathematics, biology, chemistry, and social science.

Personal Attributes

Physical therapists need to be in good physical condition, as the work involves a fair amount of lifting and other physical activity. You should have a strong desire to work with and help patients, and must have good communication skills so that you are able to relate to patients what treatments will involve. You should also be understanding and patient with the limitations of clients, and able to interact effectively with family members, as well as patients.

Requirements

Physical therapists in all states must pass a licensure exam before they can begin practicing. In addition, many states require continuing education and testing in order for a therapist to maintain his or her license. Therapists who live in states that do not require continuing education still are expected within the industry to participate. Depending on where you work, you may be required to undergo drug testing or background checks.

AT A GLANCE

Outlook

Jobs for physical therapists are expected to increase at between 21 and 37 percent through 2012, according to government reports. This is a faster growth rate than for the average job. Several factors contribute to the growth rate. There are an increasing number of elderly people in our society, and as the baby-boom generation ages, that number will continue to rise. Improvements in technology enable more babies born with birth defects to survive, often requiring extensive physical therapy treatments as the babies grow.

the person might be able to function independently at home or on the job.

Once you've thoroughly checked out the patient, you'll need to come up with a plan for treatment and how well you expect the patient will benefit. Treatments include a variety of options, such as repeated exercise, massage, electrical stimulation, hot or cold packs, and traction.

Physical therapists and physical therapist assistants teach patients the proper way to use walkers, crutches, canes, wheelchairs, and prostheses; how to move up and down steps, and how to navigate particular settings. If a patient moves from a hospital to a home setting, a physical therapist may determine whether or not home care will be necessary and lays out a plan for that care. The therapist also may inspect a patient's home to see if it's set up so the patient will be able to get around without too much trouble, and meet with family members concerning the patient's at-home care.

Physical therapists work with doctors, nurses, occupational therapists, social workers, speech therapists, teachers, school administrators, and others to determine the best course of action and treatment for each patient. Some therapists specialize in one area, such as sports medicine, cardiopulmonary therapy, or pediatrics, while others work with a variety of patients in many settings.

Pitfalls

If you decide to be a physical therapist, you're looking at a long educational path, which requires significant commitments of both time and money. As with almost any job in the medical profession, physical therapy is challenging on a number of levels. While the work itself is difficult, you also face the emotional aspects of the job, including having patients you've been working with die. The work can be discouraging if patients don't try as hard as you'd like them to, or if they can't meet the goals you've set.

Perks

Most physical therapists find their work to be both challenging and rewarding. Helping to rehabilitate someone who's been in an accident, had a stroke, or suffered another misfortune is gratifying. Physical therapists are respected within the medical community, which is reflected by their salaries. However, most physical therapists don't enter the profession looking to get rich, but to have the opportunity to work with patients who need their help and expertise.

Get a Jump on the Job

Start learning the basics of anatomy and how joints, muscles, tendons, and other body parts work as early as you can. Because educational requirements for

Joan Morse, physical therapist

Joan Morse has been a physical therapist for a long time, and she's seen her share of successes and frustrations. A veteran of nursing homes, management, and physical training for more than 10 years for a large, contract rehabilitation agency, today she teaches in a physical therapist assistant program in Fort Pierce, Florida.

While she worked in many different areas of the field, Morse says her favorite aspect of working in physical therapy is watching patients respond to the programs she's designed and seeing their conditions improve. "I always really enjoyed being involved with the patients and helping them work to get back to their prior levels," Morse says. "It's very rewarding to see somebody be able to walk again after an accident, or put away her walker, or be able to get up and down the stairs again."

Although she highly recommends physical therapy as a career path, Morse warns that it is not easy. The work is difficult from an academic standpoint, she says, and, there are constant challenges once you're on the job. "Sometimes it's hard to figure out what the primary problem is," she says. "Somebody could have a muscle strain or a small fracture, and it's your job to figure out what's causing the functional issue. There are a lot of considerations that go along with nearly every patient you see."

In addition to providing physical therapy, a therapist often ends up offering emotional support for patients, as well. "You're seeing people who are sick or injured, and there's a lot of pain associated with that," Morse said. "You have to learn to be very patient, because a lot of them have issues other than their physical ones. You have to be able to feel out a patient and get a sense of what might be going on within the overall framework of his life."

Morse, who's had students in her classes who are reluctant to touch patients, says it's extremely important to get a sense of what physical therapy is all about before deciding it will be your career.

"If you don't like, or aren't comfortable being around patients who are sick or hurting, you might not want to consider physical therapy as a career," Morse says. "Some people find they're just not comfortable with that."

She urges anyone interested in physical therapy to volunteer or work in several different settings where therapists are employed. Settings and types of therapies vary dramatically, and being exposed to various situations will give you a clearer picture of what the job is like. If you work in one setting and find that you don't like it at all, try not to get discouraged. "Don't judge your experience on a situation you have in one setting," she says. "Working in a nursing home, for instance, is much different from working in a rehabilitation hospital or a school."

If you think that the requirements to become a physical therapist are too stringent, you can always consider the job of a physical therapist assistant, which normally requires an associate's degree instead of a master's degree or doctorate.

"There are a lot of opportunities at various levels in this field," she says. "If you're interested in physical therapy, I'd advise you to explore your options."

physical therapists are stringent, consider looking into dual-enrollment with a local community college when you reach high school age and trying to get some of your general educational courses out of the way. If that's not possible, you might consider doing summer academic work before entering college.

Get all the experience you can by volunteering or working as an aide in different facilities such as nursing homes, schools, or adult day care centers. Being exposed to different types of patients and medical environments will help you to decide whether or not you're comfortable working in that type of situation.

SCIENTIFIC INVENTOR

OVERVIEW

Take a minute to look around the room you happen to be in. Do you see a light? A computer? A ballpoint pen? A paper clip? Each of those items—as well as millions more—started out as an idea hatched by an inventor. Aspirin, automobiles, air conditioners, iPods, DVD players, video games, digital cameras, printing presses, and super-stick glue are all the inventions of creative people, just like you.

Unfortunately, there are lots of good ideas that, for one reason or another, never get off the ground. There are also a lot of ideas that result in products that end up taking up space in the inventor's house because there's no market for them. That's not to say, however, that you can't be a successful inventor.

The trick is to educate yourself about the process of inventing before actually moving ahead with your idea. There are certain steps you need to take before you start investing time and energy into your proposed invention.

If you have a great idea, the first step to take is to make sure somebody else didn't have it first. Check out applicable Web sites, stores, catalogs, or any other place you can think of that offers items similar to the one you have in mind. If you don't see anything like what you have in mind, then you can move on to conducting a patent search. This will tell you if anyone has applied for a patent for a product that is the same, or similar, to what you're planning.

AT A GLANCE

Salary Range

An inventor's salary depends on the invention and how the product is marketed and received. Dean Kamen, whose inventions include a mobile dialysis system, a new type of heart stent, an all-terrain wheelchair, and the Segway Human Transporter, is a multimillionaire who lives in a mansion on his own island and owns a fleet of helicopters. Other inventors, however, never earn any monetary reward.

Education/Experience

Anyone can be an inventor without any education, but traditionally inventors find an engineering or science background helpful. Kamen attended Worcester Polytechnic Institute in Massachusetts, but never finished. Ideally, you should have a strong educational background in the area of what you plan to invent.

Personal Attributes

Inventors are creative, free thinking, and extremely determined. You may have to work on your invention for years to get it right, and then face an uphill battle to get it properly marketed and available. You should be able to "think outside the box," and to act on your ideas. You also should have good marketing ideas and skills so that you can get your invention to the public once it's been completed.

Requirements

You'll need to protect your invention, and the type of protection you'll need depends on what you invent. The United States Patent and Trademark office has very definite rules about obtaining and keeping patents, so you'll need to find out how the rules apply to your particular invention.

Outlook

There is always demand for new products, or room to improve on existing products. As long as these demands continue, there will be a market for inventors.

If you're thorough, you can conduct a pretty good patent search on your own. You'll need to go to the United States Patent and Trademark Office Web site (http://www.uspto.gov) and search by entering any word you can think of that describes the product you plan to invent. Make sure you use the "classification" and

Ray Booska, scientific inventor

Ray Booska of West Melbourne, Florida, wasn't looking for a new career when a friend told him about a company with which he was planning to get involved. The company manufactured vests designed to provide cooling for firefighters, soldiers, construction workers, and others who work in very hot conditions. "A friend told me about this cool-vest company, and I thought it sounded interesting," Booska says. "I was doing something altogether different at that point."

Soon, Booska too got involved with the company. There were some problems involving the existing product, however, and Booska and his partner decided to go back to square one. With permission from the original inventor, they reexamined the technology, and came up with a better way of making the cooling vests. "We improved on the technology and, basically, we invented a better mousetrap," Booska says.

The vest, called the Original Cool Vest, uses a material designed to absorb the heat generated by the person wearing it. The vest temperature stays at 59 degrees, which keeps the wearer cool without freezing, as would some models of ice or gel-cooled clothing.

Vests made using the new technology were very well received, and Booska found himself with a rapidly growing business. His company, called Glacier Tek, Inc., manufactures the vests, which are used by the military, law enforcement personnel, fire and rescue workers, in foundries and industrial safety industries, and in petrochemical processing. They also are popular with those involved with motor sports and motorcycling, sports participants, hunting, fishing, and other outdoor activities.

In the 10 years since Booska and his partner invented the new technology and started making the new-and-improved vests, they've moved to a larger facility and then expanded again. They now have distribution partners all across the United States and in Australia, the United Kingdom, Japan, and Canada. They expect to soon also have distributors in Greece, Turkey, Israel, and Kuwait.

The newest product to employ this technology is a cool vest for military dogs trained to sniff out bombs in war zones. That was especially rewarding for Booska and his partner, both of whom served in the military. Booska used his own pet (a retired, 100-pound police dog) as a model for the canine cool vest. The company donated the first vests to military dogs in Afghanistan and Iraq, where they were quickly put to use. "Now the dogs can stay out for two hours at a time without becoming overheated," he says. Police departments with K-9 units also have purchased vests for their dogs.

Booska advised anyone who has a good idea they wish to develop to learn all you can about the type of product you want to develop and the process of inventing. And, he says, be prepared to stick with it, because chances are that you'll need to try, try, and then try again. "It's a combination of brain power, education, and persistence," Booska says.

"invention by year" search tools as well as the general search. If you've already made tons of money from an invention, or you just happen to have a lot of money at your disposal, you can hire your own patent attorney to conduct a search.

To protect your invention, you'll need to get a patent (or another form of protection, depending on the type of invention). A utility patent is needed if your invention is something that people will use. If you have an idea for a slogan or logo, you'll need a trademark.

Once you're rolling along with your idea for a great invention, it's very important to protect yourself so nobody else can come along and steal it. It may sound odd, but you should be very careful with whom you discuss your idea, and you should have every person you do discuss it with sign a nondisclosure agreement. That means they agree not to act on or use your idea. You can write your own agreement, or check out one of the legal sites on the Internet that lets you print out free forms.

Before you start building your better mousetrap, try to figure out what you'll do with it once it's been built. You can set up a stand in front of your house, but you probably won't get rich from having your neighbors buying the product. You'll need to figure out how the product will be manufactured and distributed. Most stores won't buy a product from an individual who has only one product to offer, no matter how great it is. They may, however, buy it from a manufacturer who has other products to offer, in addition to yours.

If you give a manufacturer permission to make and sell your product, you're licensing the product. In turn, you'll receive a commission, or royalty, on each item sold.

As you can see, there's more to being an inventor than just heading down to the basement and turning your great idea into a saleable product. You'll need to do a lot of reading, learning, and planning before you're ready to become the next Dean Kamen or Bill Gates.

Pitfalls

Inventors sometimes invest huge amounts of time and effort into developing an idea, only to find out that it's already been done, or that someone else has a patent and has never used it, or that there's really no market for the idea after all. Inventors sometimes fall prey to dishonest swindlers who steal their ideas and claim them as their own. Getting an invention to market can be complicated, and it can be expensive to hire lawyers to guide you through the process.

Perks

What could be better than taking your own original idea and turning it into a useful, usable, important product that people will use? Inventors gain recognition, and, if your invention is well received and useful to many people, you could make a lot of money.

Get a Jump on the Job

The first thing to do, in addition to reading all you can about being an inventor, is to start a journal that chronicles your idea and everything you do to act on that idea. There are a lot of guidelines concerning an inventor's journal. It's got to be in the proper type of book, the entries must not have any spaces in between them, every entry must be clearly dated, and it must include the names of everyone who you talk to about your invention. There are a lot more regulations, so you'll need to get a book or go on the Internet to learn more.

SET MEDIC

OVERVIEW

The actors are assembled, the clapper loader is poised, the director is ready to start the action, when suddenly a cry goes up—one of the child actors just got a splinter! Where's the medic? Get the medic!

Everything grinds to a halt as the set medic appears, Band-Aid and salve to the rescue—just another patient in the medic's busy day on the set.

Whenever a cast and crew assembles to film a commercial, a film, or a TV show, a medic is almost always required to be on hand to provide for the medical needs of everybody on the set. The medic is also the safety liaison between the production and construction crews and various government agencies responsible for on-the-job safety. Set medics are responsible for handling all the workers' comp paperwork, handling all the work-related injuries, and dealing with documentation on unsafe working conditions.

Days may go by and the set medic may get nothing more serious to attend to than a headache or a case of hives. But should an elderly actor suddenly double over with a heart attack, the set medic's presence can spell the difference between life or death.

A wide range of medical personnel can serve as a set medic—either an emergency medical technician (EMT), a paramedic, a nurse, or even a physician—but regardless of the credentials, the pay and the job responsibilities are the same. Typically, the set medic arrives from the beginning of preproduction or construction through filming or striking the set.

It's the medic's job to provide immediate medical attention in case of accidents or illness—and there are hazards everywhere: electrical wires, props, and machinery litter the soundstage. On location, other dangers appear. There's the risk of moving cars, temporary ramps, speeding trains. Going on location may entail its own risks—set medics might find themselves out in the middle of the desert, in the middle of the ocean, or in a remote jungle arena.

As in most areas of the entertainment scene—especially in Hollywood—landing your first job as a set medic takes time, perseverance, and knowing the right people. Most jobs are also union in Hollywood, which creates its own difficulties. Once you've received your EMT or nursing license and you decide you want to be a set medic, you've got to spend about $300 to buy your own equipment for basic life support and nonprescription medications. It may take several years of working small jobs before you're able to join the union, which will bring you lots more work—but when you do, initiation fees can top $2,600. Once you're a member of the union, you can either leave your name with your union as an available medic or work as an independent contractor.

Unlike many professions in the entertainment business, being a set medic is an

Wayne Fielder, set medic

As a child Wayne Fielder dreamed of being in the medical profession, but once he became an adult he found himself working in the restaurant business, training as a chef and owning his own place. As the years went by, however, he never got over his yearning for a medical career. At the age of 35, he decided to go for training as an emergency medical technician.

After nine years as an EMT, a friend suggested he consider working as a set medic in Hollywood. "A lot of people don't know this job even exists," he says. "I always kind of wanted to be next to show business, so this was the perfect job for me."

The hard part is getting started, since these jobs are almost all unionized. It may take a year or two to meet all of the requirements for union membership and actually get called for a job as a set medic. "It's always better when you know somebody on the inside," Fielder says, "but if you're persistent, you can get in on your own." After submitting his resume outlining his medical experience to the motion picture first aid union (IATSE, local 767), he waited for more than a year and a half to get work. Eventually, he got called for that first job, and he's never looked back. "You need to schmooze with everyone," Fielder says. "You need to be very likeable, very courteous on the set. If they like you, they'll call you more often." As he worked on various sets, he passed out his business cards to everybody he met. "People use you for a day here, a day there. You establish your own name. Once you make friends, you network with each other and you just continuously bounce work off each other."

It's certainly not like working in an emergency room or going out to the scene of accidents. "Very rarely is there any trauma," Fielder notes. What there is, is a lot of perks. "A friend of mine [did] *Pirates of the Caribbean II* with Johnny Depp," Fielder says. "They pay for all his meals, hotel rooms. They fly in his family when he goes on location to the Caribbean." You also get to meet famous directors and actors. "There are some very nice actors," he says. "Some are there to work and don't want to be bothered. For the most part, they're happy making $20 million a picture. They know you're there as an hourly employee just trying to do your best."

The job is 50 percent skill, 50 percent courtesy, he says. "You'll be with big-name actors and actresses. Most of the time you are doing absolutely nothing. You have a walkie-talkie during production, and if they need you for any reason they will call you, so you don't have to sit in one location."

Another perk is the salary—there's no doubt that the money is very, very good. In addition to top union wages, if you're called to work as a set medic, you're guaranteed eight hours. If

(continues)

(continued)

the actor or foreman doesn't show up, you can go home—but you're still paid for eight hours. If you're working on a feature film or program, the company is required to feed you a full meal every six hours, or else they'll have to pay a "meal penalty" of $12.50 an hour added to your wages for every 15 minutes they're late with your lunch. "It's amazing the money they actually throw away," Fielder says. "Many people in Hollywood tend to be very spoiled, but I thank every day I'm blessed with this job. When I started on the ambulance, I was making $6.50 an hour. So I'm really thankful to be doing this."

Ideally, Fielder likes to work for three months and then take a month off. "Usually you do a film or TV show, and when that wraps, you're out of work." Of course, once you're out of work, you're eligible for unemployment until the next gig comes along.

Basically, working on a movie set is pretty tame—at least compared to answering 911 calls. "I haven't even come close to anything I've seen in the field," he says. Still, there are sometimes fatalities or serious injuries on some sets; such as a decapitation on the first *Spider-Man* film. "You might not do anything for six months, but that one time an elderly actor has a heart attack or some electrical worker falls off a scaffolding, you have to be ready for that," he says. "You get a lot of allergic reactions, lots of splinters during construction—mostly just first aid."

If there are any life-threatening emergencies, Fielder calls 911. "I can stabilize the patient before the ambulance arrives, but really so far I've not had anything major. But you have to be ready."

In the end, it can be satisfying—and you also get to see your name in lights. "I like to see my name in the credits," Fielder confesses. "I get to meet movie stars, I'm a little nosy. I've always thought that people in the movies seemed untouchable, but they're just people."

The only thing he doesn't like about the job are the hours and the responsibility. "Sometimes you might be doing a film in the Mohave desert taking care of a crew in the middle of the desert in the middle of the summer. It's your responsibility to keep everyone hydrated, to carry electrolyte tablets, provide sunscreen. Whatever the conditions, it might be hot, it might be rainy—you've got to keep 'em healthy. That's your job."

Often, it's the set medic's job to keep the actors going. "Their philosophy is: 'There is no tomorrow. We've got to get this done today. Time is money.' So if an actor gets a bump, you wrap it up and send 'em back in, as horrible as it may seem. You do the best you can to stabilize them if it's a nonthreatening emergency. Maybe you can send them to a doctor afterwards. You have to use your best judgment."

In the end, it's a very rewarding job. "When you wrap, after doing a whole movie, you've bonded with the crew, 15 hours a day, it's your family."

Some medics sit in their office and wait to get called, but Fielder likes to be seen around the set, and the actors often come up to him for advice. "On the set, you're the doc, the psychiatrist," he says. "They neglect themselves and say: 'Can you look at my back? Can you lance this for me?' Then you recommend they see the doctor."

"Being a set medic is a wonderful alternative, an excellent job. I wish I'd known about this job years ago," Fielder says. "I wouldn't have been breaking my back on the freeway handling traffic accidents."

equal opportunity job—equally accessible to both men and women of all ages. You can make yourself even more marketable by getting scuba certification so you can be available during underwater filming, or by getting certified to operate an automatic defibrillator, so you can carry your own device. Getting a pediatric certification will allow you to work with infants used on a film or a show.

Pitfalls

It can be a long, hard slog to break into the business and start getting jobs, and once you do, the hours can be quite long, especially for set medics on location during a movie shoot. Going on location could mean you're away from home for two or three months.

Perks

The pay is top notch, the perks are terrific (lots of great catered food, plenty of snacks, and very little to do most of the time). If you're working on a film, going on location can mean you're sent to a beautiful spot anywhere in the world, with food and lodging paid for. If you're away for several months, the company may pay to fly your family in to visit. If you're a film buff, working on a set with movie stars and famous individuals can be fun as well.

Get a Jump on the Job

If you want to be a set medic someday, you've first got to get a job and some experience in the medical field. In most states, you can become an EMT at the age of 18; once you're certified, you can go out on calls to see if this is the sort of thing you like to do. Some towns will let you become a first aid attendant or ambulance corps volunteer at 14 or 16. Check the various volunteer service organizations in your town to see how you can help, and if this is the type of career in which you might be interested. After a few years of experience as an EMT, you may be ready to try your luck as a set medic. Of course, you can also become a nurse (or even a doctor) first, and then move into the set medic field. Those careers obviously require much more schooling and experience.

VENOM RESEARCHER

OVERVIEW

Deadly snakes, poisonous sea creatures, harmful insects—all carrying death with one swift bite. But the venom that kills can also save lives—and that's where a venom researcher comes in. Venom can be used to develop antivenin (the medicine that can save your life if you get bitten by a poisonous creature.) But there's lots more to venom than just its poison: The toxic compounds it contains may also yield new drugs to treat everything from crippling strokes to deadly heart attacks.

Snake venom is a complicated stew containing all sorts of compounds, which are basically divided into two groups— neurotoxins and hemotoxins. Neurotoxins attack the central nervous system, so that the victim's muscles stop working and the victim suffocates. Hemotoxins affect the circulatory system, leading to uncontrolled bleeding. Snakes known to employ neurotoxic venom are a deadly bunch, including cobras, coral snakes, kraits, and sea snakes. Snakes whose toxins are filled with hemotoxins include rattlesnakes, copperheads, and cottonmouths.

But venom researchers spend lots of time studying snake venom not just to develop antivenin, but to try to uncover new medicines to help fight disease. It may seem odd that something so deadly could also heal, but it's a fact. Once a scientist has accumulated venom, it's analyzed; promising compounds are then reproduced synthetically.

AT A GLANCE

Salary Range

Salary varies widely depending on the size and location of the institution where the researcher works and whether the researcher also has teaching responsibilities (most do). Salaries can range from a low of $57,564 to significantly above $92,000, depending on rank. In addition, many researchers who are also faculty members have significant earnings in addition to their base salary from consulting, teaching additional courses, research, writing for publication, or other employment with pharmaceutical companies or independent businesses.

Education/Experience

A college education with an emphasis in the sciences (especially biology, biochemistry, and chemistry) is required; a Ph.D. is recommended, either in chemistry or pharmacology. It is important not to neglect other studies as well—you'll need courses in statistics, computer science, writing, and foreign languages.

Personal Attributes

Patience, a great sense of curiosity, a certain fearlessness, ability to work alone.

Requirements

You'll need a Ph.D. in some related science to do research at the university level, where you'll probably also teach courses.

Outlook

Good. Research into possible medicinal uses of venom make this a growing field as drug companies search for new drugs with fewer side effects.

Scientists are currently studying neurotoxins to treat some brain injuries, strokes, or Alzheimer's disease; in one special area of interest, venom researchers are

Jon-Paul Bingham, venom researcher

When it comes to figuring out how to make drugs from slugs, venom researcher Jon-Paul Bingham is one of the world's best. Bingham, a biochemist at Clarkson University in New York, started out wanting to be a veterinarian in his native Australia. But growing up in a country known for its astonishing number of venomous creatures, his interest veered off into toxicology. "You have a country that will eat, bite, sting, and make a meal of you very quickly and easily," he laughs. "In Australia where I come from, we are in constant contact—unwillingly—with venomous creatures. So the clinical understanding of how these toxins and venoms work is very important, specifically in the treatment of bite victims."

In his final undergraduate year at college, he was offered a research project on cone-shell toxins. Cone snails harpoon their prey with pointed, needle-like tongues, which inject potent toxins to immobilize prey. As part of the project, he'd actually get to collect the shells. "Scuba diving was one of my loves and passions. This, in turn, fed my hobby of shell collecting. I collect shells and I specialized in—you guessed it—cone shells.

"Realizing that this area of research regarding the cone shells was poorly understood and that most scientists had never seen a live specimen, I thought it would be a good idea to learn more about what these venomous creatures could do," he says, "and use my combined skills as a scuba diver and shell collector to study these venomous snails as a living organism, not just as a dried powder of biological toxins." For the past 15 years, he's been doing just that.

"They are actually one of the most advanced marine venomous organisms in the world," he says. There are more than 600 known cone snail species, which inhabit the world's dwindling coral reefs. Each is able to produce more than 100 types of toxins, and each one of those toxins is a potential lifesaving drug. "All drugs, no matter for what use, they all have a therapeutic index," Bingham says. "They become beneficial or toxic depending on the dose. So with a toxic cone shell, if we can use the toxins it has at a smaller dose—in that therapeutic range—we can make a toxin into a drug."

It may sound easy, but the hard part is that each toxin is filled with compounds that could be of potential use. "We have so many compounds [from the cone shell toxin]—at least 75,000 compounds. The issue is trying to home in which ones we can use in a clinical or drug application. It may take us many years to get to a bottle of drugs based on that compound."

Cone shells range from thumb- to foot-size, but most fit into the palm of your hand. It's the very beauty of the shell that intrigued Dr. Bingham. "They have been collected for hundreds of years," he says, "and even Rembrandt painted pictures of cone shells. They are very well known in the art world and in the world of amateur collectors." An avid scuba diver, Dr. Bingham collects cone shells in tropical waters for his research. "I've dined with cannibals and ex-headhunters," he says. "I've dined with princes and kings and queens in the South Pacific Islands. As a researcher who does this type of work—why, the world is my laboratory. I can do my work and take my snails and bring back the compounds, but the fun part is to be able to see the world in a different perspective, to leave behind the luxuries and see the world. You go to

(continues)

Hawaii, and you meet people who help you collect these snails. They are proud to be helping the medical process."

As a naturalist as well as a scientist, Dr. Bingham is well aware of the delicate balance that exists in the universe, especially when it comes to the tropical reefs that the cone shell calls home. Cone snails are found primarily in coral reefs in warm, tropical waters, but about 26 percent of the world's reefs are damaged beyond repair, and another 30 to 50 percent are severely degraded. "There are people who are going to the South Pacific to collect these shells who are not very well aware of the potential damage to a reef system or a single population of cone shells, and that's very worrisome to me," he says. "We have created a biosustainable process in which we bring only a few specimens back, keeping them happy in captivity for many years."

Instead of killing the snails for their venom, Dr. Bingham has learned how to obtain the toxin by milking them much like other experts milk snakes. "Discoveries have to start somewhere," he says. Dr. Bingham is starting right at the beginning, trying to understand the snail as a whole organism. "In turn, this will provide us a more in-depth knowledge as to why these slugs have developed the use of toxins and why they have so many of them. By understanding the diversity of these toxins, maybe we will discover more uses for them."

The toxins in cone shells (conotoxins) block key pathways and have been shown to be effective in the diagnosis and possible treatment of small-cell lung cancer. Another compound now in clinical trials also has a powerful antiepileptic effect; still other research suggests that conotoxins could treat muscle spasticity, and prevent cell death when there is inadequate circulation, such as during strokes, head injuries, or coronary bypass surgery. Studies indicate they could be used to treat depression and heart arrhythmias, too. But it's as a painkiller that these snail venoms have generated huge excitement. The first conotoxin to be approved by the U.S. Food and Drug Administration is Prialt, which is so specific in the way it acts in the body, that it's a thousand times more potent than morphine.

"There is an enormous level of interest to discover more types of these drugs," Dr. Bingham says. "We use nature as an original template and learn from nature how we can use these compounds to combat a variety of disease. My specialty is in cardiovascular disease. With the toxins we have, we can delicately dissect receptors in the heart which no one else has ever been able to do."

Because so few people know how to feed or breed cone snails, the importance of his job lies in farming the snails so that scientists will no longer need to use destructive processes to obtain the venoms from inside the shells.

"As a scientist, where else could I have a job like this, to make a contribution to society, to have the freedom to do what I want to do, to work with friends and colleagues—you could call it the best little job in the world. I can't think of a time where I've ever thought of throwing in the towel. Every time I turn a corner, there's another question to be asked, and we don't have an answer. By doing basic research, maybe we'll get answers and through those answers, we may get to the stage of being able to design better drugs from cone shells themselves. I love my job as an educator, researcher, and a mentor," Bingham says. "The students I teach see my passion for this work, and this rubs off on them. To see that they get it, that they understand science, is very rewarding."

assessing the blood thinning compounds in venom, which might one day be used to help treat patients with heart attacks or blood disorders.

Other scientists are studying sea snake venom in hopes of finding toxins that target particular brain cells involved in learning and memory. This could lead to new insights into dementia, which might lead to new treatments.

Because a number of toxins found in venom have evolved so they can target specific vital processes in the body, they seem to be a lot more selective than many drugs now on the market. This has led scientists to figure out how to transform some portions of the toxins into new medications. For example, Aggrastat is a kind of super aspirin that prevents blood clots. Scientists hope the new medicine might be able to help prevent heart attacks in certain individuals.

Other venom researchers are studying a compound from copperhead venom to help fight breast cancer, and a chemical from a Malayan pit viper that might treat stroke. Cobra venom may one day be used to help treat Parkinson's disease.

But snakes aren't the only poisonous creatures that venom researchers study. Poisonous frogs and sea creatures, such as cone shells, also provide their own share of helpful pharmacology hidden within deadly toxins.

While there are more than 600 cone shell species in the world, some of them inject their victims with a toxic liquid filled with conotoxins, which are so deadly they can paralyze their prey in seconds. Humans who have picked up one of these shells have sometimes died without even realizing they'd been stung. Cone shell venom may contain more than 50,000 conotoxins, at least 50 of which can target the brain and nervous system. Venom researchers have isolated more than 100 specific toxins that may one day be used to treat a wide range of diseases from arthritis to cancer. The very first new drug to be synthesized from a conotoxin is a painkiller (Prialt) 1,000 times stronger than morphine.

Pitfalls

Many venom researchers milk snakes to obtain the venom, which inevitably leads to bites. Some researchers have been bitten hundreds of times—which is almost always painful and can be deadly.

Perks

For venom researchers, the lure of their job is in its mystery and exciting possibilities—there really are incredible treatments hiding in the most toxic places, and these scientists are on the verge of enormous discoveries. What could be more rewarding than that? Also, many venom researchers travel to exotic places to find venoms.

Get a Jump on the Job

Perhaps you're already a budding herpetologist—or maybe you just love chemistry and biology. Read everything you can about poisons, toxins, and toxic creatures. Visit the zoo and study the toxic creatures. Consider an internship and take every biology and chemistry course you can.

VIROLOGIST

OVERVIEW

Just about every day, it seems there's a new virus in the news that threatens human health: Lyme disease. Bird flu. West Nile virus.

The scientist whose job it is to keep up with these new and emerging organisms is called a virologist. As new viruses emerge, virologists scramble to understand the virus, stop it from spreading, and learn how to treat it. This is extremely important work, because a virus that cannot be controlled could be a worldwide threat.

You'll find virologists at work in the government, at colleges and universities, hospitals, pharmaceutical companies, diagnostic laboratories, biotechnology firms, industrial laboratories, agricultural-related businesses, and food and beverage companies. While some virologists are hired to work full time, others are hired on a contract basis to conduct an individual research project. This is often the method for a company trying to come up with a vaccine for a particular virus. Some virologists depend on funding from grants for their projects; others split their time teaching and conducting research.

Scientists have long struggled to understand and control viruses, which range from the 130 types of the common cold to deadly viruses such as Ebola and AIDS. Viruses can be transmitted through the air, through blood or body fluids, or via person-to-person contact. Infected needles used to inject drugs also can spread viruses.

Virologists who work with dangerous viruses must take special pains to

AT A GLANCE

Salary Range

The average salary for a virologist is $68,262, according to government statistics.

Education/Experience

You'll need at least a bachelor of science degree, but that probably will only qualify you for a non-research job or a position as a laboratory assistant or technician. Most virologists have a least a master's degree, and the majority have earned Ph.D.s.

Personal Attributes

You should be inquisitive, able to think creatively, and have the patience to persevere for long periods of time to figure out a problem or come up with the answer to a question. You should enjoy the process of scientific research, be precise, and well organized. You must also have the ability to communicate your findings, both orally and in writing.

Requirements

Depending on where you work and the nature of your work, you may need security clearances.

Outlook

Jobs in virology are expected to increase at an average rate, between 10 and 20 percent through 2012.

protect themselves from being exposed to the organisms. They may wear protective clothing and work in restricted areas to avoid contamination.

Virologists often work with other scientists, such as immunologists or bacteriologists, to conduct research that examines the properties of viruses and the microorganisms that cause them. They will work under controlled conditions to isolate the virus and place it into a culture, where it can be carefully analyzed. Virologists may also conduct tests to determine if dangerous viral infections are found in food sources, water, and the environment.

Although you may be able to get a job as a virologist with just a bachelor's degree, you won't be able to advance in the field. A master's degree may qualify you to conduct experiments in a laboratory setting. However, in order to be qualified to teach at a university, manage a diagnostic

Dr. Preston A. Marx, virologist

If you spend a fair amount of time reading and sending e-mail, you have something in common with Dr. Preston A. Marx, who's been a virologist for more than 25 years. While your e-mails might deal with homework assignments or plans for the weekend, however, Marx corresponds with other scientists and is involved in ongoing experiments and projects.

"The colleagues I work with are all over the country and all over the world," Marx says. "I spend a lot of time with my e-mail, corresponding with other scientists."

Marx is a professor of tropical medicine at the Tulane University Health Sciences Center in New Orleans, but he doesn't spend much time teaching. About 95 percent of his working hours are spent on research projects, most of which focus on the HIV and SIV viruses. SIV—simian immunodeficiency virus—is the monkey's version of the HIV virus (the virus that causes AIDS). He works out of the Tulane Regional Primate Research Centers, one of eight national primate research centers across the country.

Marx is fascinated by viruses, and committed to continuing the research that enables him to learn all he can about them. While medical personnel and those in certain other disciplines consider disease from the patient's point of view, Marx always views it from the virus' viewpoint. "Virologists view the world through the eyes of the virus," Marx says. "We want to know where it came from, how it evolved, what genes it uses. We want to know everything we can about it."

Marx is well known and respected as a virologist specializing in HIV and SIV research, and is highly regarded as a lecturer on the origin of HIV and HIV vaccines. He's published more than 190 research articles, nearly all dealing with AIDS and HIV. His research frequently takes him to Africa, where he is studying the origin and spread of the viruses.

"We must find out where these new viruses come from," Marx says. "We've got to understand why some viruses fail and why some don't." The answers to those questions lie in systematic, step-by-step research that could take years, or even decades. "It's like being Sherlock Holmes," Marx says.

He feels fortunate to be able to spend so much time in research, a luxury not afforded to many virologists. Most university virologists split their time about 50-50 between teaching and research, he says. He recommends that anyone interested in becoming a virologist should earn a bachelor's degree in a biological science, such as biology, zoology, microbiology, or immunology. Graduate school is extremely important, he advises, and a Ph.D. will take you much further than a master's degree. "A Ph.D. really gives you the background to do what virologists do," Marx says.

Modern communication methods have revolutionized the work of virologists, who now can send samples and results back and forth with very little time lag. "I work with colleagues across the country the way I used to work with colleagues down the hall," Marx says.

virology laboratory at a hospital, lead research projects, or advance to senior positions in government or industry, you'll need to earn a Ph.D.

Virology is an extremely important field, and virologists are well regarded in the scientific community. They often come under pressure from employers who are anxious to learn more about a particular virus or to get a vaccine on the market to combat it. Virologists often work long hours, especially when they're facing research or development deadlines.

Pitfalls

It takes a significant educational commitment to earn the degrees necessary for a top job in the field of virology. That means it will be expensive, and you may find yourself starting out with a large amount of debt. Once you get a job, you're likely to find that the hours are long, and you'll be under pressure to meet stringent deadlines. Also, you'll probably find yourself working with some scary, and potentially deadly viruses, which can be risky if you're not extremely careful.

Perks

Working as a virologist provides the opportunity to conduct important work that can benefit people and animals around the world. You get to work with other scientists to solve problems that could result in extremely detrimental circumstances. And virologists generally earn a good deal of money and enjoy the respect of their colleagues and students.

Get a Jump on the Job

Begin by studying everything you can about how different viruses have evolved and how they've been treated. Take all the science courses that you can, particularly in the biological field. If you live near a college or university with a strong science department, see if you can access the faculty directory. If there's a virologist on staff, you may be able to e-mail him or her and ask for advice and direction.

APPENDIX A: ASSOCIATIONS, ORGANIZATIONS, AND WEB SITES

ACUPUNCTURIST

The Accreditation Commission for Acupuncture and Oriental Medicine
7501 Greenway Center Drive, Suite 820
Greenbelt, MD 20770
(301) 313-0855
info.md@acaom.org
http://www.acaom.org

The Accreditation Commission for Acupuncture and Oriental Medicine (ACAOM) was founded in 1982 by the Council of Colleges of Acupuncture and Oriental Medicine. It serves as an independent body to evaluate available certificate and diploma programs, and serves as an accreditation board for schools in the United States which offer · programs in acupuncture and other areas of Oriental medicine. There are more than 50 schools in the United States that have been accredited or have candidacy status with the ACAOM.

The National Certification Commission for Acupuncture and Oriental Medicine
11 Canal Center Plaza, Suite 300
Alexandria, VA 22314
(703) 548-9004
info@nccaom.org
http://www.nccaom.org

The National Certification Commission for Acupuncture and Oriental Medicine (NCCAOM) is a nonprofit organization with a mission to establish and promote high standards of safety and reliability in acupuncture and other areas of Oriental medicine. The agency is a member of the National Organization for Competency Assurance, and is accredited by the National Commission for Certifying Agencies. Thirty-two states and the District of Columbia require NCCAOM certification in order to work in that state or district as an acupuncturist. The NCCAOM's certification process is stringent, including hands-on and written test components. Since it was established in 1982, NCCAOM has certified more than 13,000 acupuncturists, Chinese herbologists, and Asian bodywork therapists.

AROMATHERAPIST

The Aromatherapist USA
http://www.thearomatherapistusa.com
Web site for aromatherapists.

Aromatherapy Registration Council
5940 SW Hood Avenue
Portland, OR 97039
(503) 244-0276
info@aromatherapycouncil.org
http://www.aromatherapycouncil.org

The registration council sponsors a voluntary examination to test the core body of knowledge that is aromatherapy at the present time (assuming that a core body of knowledge could be determined), with an emphasis on public safety.

Ashi Therapy
PO Box 1858
Banner Elk, NC 28604

(828) 898-5555

http://www.ashitherapy.com

This healing center is located in the Blue Ridge Mountains in the northwest corner of North Carolina. The Center offers holistic alternative therapies and traditional Chinese medicine, acupuncture, qigong, reiki, acupressure, shiatsu, reflexology, aromatherapy, massage, aromatic detox body wraps, Chinese facial rejuvenation, and a complete herbal pharmacy including Bach flower remedies, essential oils, music, books, gifts, classes, and workshops.

National Association for Holistic Aromatherapy

3327 W. Indian Trail Road PMB 144

Spokane, WA 99208

(509)325-3419

http://www.naha.org

This educational, nonprofit organization is dedicated to enhancing public awareness of the benefits of true aromatherapy. NAHA is actively involved with promoting and elevating academic standards in aromatherapy education and practice for the profession. NAHA is also actively involved in furthering the public's perception and knowledge of true aromatherapy and its safe and effective application in everyday life. NAHA's mission is to revive the knowledge of the medicinal use of aromatic plants and essential oils to its fullest extent and to restore aromatherapy to a truly holistic professional art and science. NAHA is the leader in promoting and elevating true aromatherapy through the active dissemination of educational material to the general public, trade/professional

associations, business owners, and practitioners.

ART THERAPIST

American Art Therapy Association

1202 Allanson Road

Mundelein, IL 60060-3808

(888) 290-0878

info@arttherapy.org

http://www.arttherapy.org

The American Art Therapy Association (AATA), founded in 1969, is a national professional organization that sponsors annual conferences and regional symposia, approves training programs, and publishes the journal Art Therapy.

National Coalition of Creative Arts Therapies Associations

c/o AMTA

8455 Colesville Road, Suite 1000

Silver Spring, MD 20910

http://www.nccata.org

The National Coalition of Creative Arts Therapies Associations (NCCATA), founded in 1979, is an alliance of professional associations dedicated to the advancement of the arts as therapeutic modalities. NCCATA represents over 8,000 individual members of six creative arts therapies associations. The creative arts therapies include art therapy, dance/ movement therapy, drama therapy, music therapy, poetry therapy, and psychodrama. These therapies use arts modalities and creative processes during intentional intervention in therapeutic, rehabilitative, community, or educational settings to foster health, communication, and expression; promote the integration of physical, emotional, cognitive, and social functioning; enhance self-awareness; and facilitate change.

ASTRONAUT

National Aeronautics and Space Administration (NASA)
NASA Headquarters
Suite 1M32
Washington, DC 20546-0001
(202) 358-0001
public-inquiries@hq.nasa.gov
http://www.nasa.gov

Since it was established in 1958, NASA has focused on scientific research and in stimulating public interest in aerospace exploration, as well as science and technology in general.

ASTRONOMER

The American Astronomical Society
2000 Florida Avenue, NW, Suite 400
Washington, DC 20009-1231
(202) 328-2010
aas@aas.org
http://www.aas.org

The American Astronomical Society was founded in 1899 to promote the advancement of astronomy and other, relevant areas of science. With about 6,500 members from the areas of astronomy, physics, mathematics, engineering, geology, and others, it sponsors association-wide meetings, offers grants and prizes for members, and educational opportunities. It also publishes three scientific journals, a newsletter for members, and other publications. The association offers several summer opportunities for college

students who are involved in studying astronomy.

The National Optical Astronomy Observatory
950 North Cherry Avenue
Tucson, AZ 85726
outreach@noao.edu
http://www.noao.edu

The National Optical Astronomy Observatory (NOAO) is a consolidation of astronomical observatories managed by the Association of Universities for Research in Astronomy (AURA). The member observatories are: Kitt Peak National Observatory, located near Tucson, Arizona; the Cerro Tololo Inter-American Observatory in northern Chile; and the National Solar Observatory, which has facilities in New Mexico and Arizona. NOAO operates under cooperative agreement with the National Science Foundation. Astronomers from all over the world come to NOAO facilities to access the top-rate equipment and research opportunities. Aspiring astronomers can visit and get tours of the facilities, and can access the Web site, which contains reports on current research, information about astronomy, and links to other sites.

CRIME SCENE EXAMINER

Federal Law Enforcement Officers Association
PO Box 326
Lewisberry, PA 17339
(717) 938-2300
services@fleoa.org
http://www.fleoa.org

FLEOA is the largest nonpartisan professional organization representing only federal law enforcement officers. It represents more than 20,000 federal agents from more than 50 different agencies. The association was founded in 1977 mainly to provide legal help to federal officers. FLEOA also tries to encourage legislation that benefits federal agents. The association has helped to increase death benefits, provide scholarships for children of officers killed in the line of duty, helped raise pay scales and encouraged passage of a bill that makes federal officers eligible for a Congressional Medal of Honor. The association's officers are active duty federal agents who are required to conduct association business while they are off duty or on leave.

Fraternal Order of Police
1410 Donelson Pike, Suite A-17
Nashville, TN 37217
(615) 399-0900
glfop@grandlodgefop.org
http://grandlodgefop.org

Founded in 1915, the Fraternal Order of Police (FOP) is an organization of more than 321,000 members, all of whom are sworn law enforcement officers. There also is a civilian affiliate of the FOP and an FOP auxiliary organization. The FOP speaks for all those who work in law enforcement, working to improve safety for officers, and to provide education. It represents police on legislative matters and provides employee representation, when necessary.

(614) 292-9207
asc41@infinet.com
http://www.asc41.com

The American Society of Criminology (ASC) is an international organization concerned with bringing together the multiple disciplines within the field of criminology for study, research, and education. The society is broken down into specialized divisions, including Corrections and Sentencing, Critical Criminology, Women and Crime, International Criminology, and People of Color and Crime. Each division, as well as the ASC in general publishes journals and newsletters for members. The ASC holds an annual meeting and sponsors periodical calls for papers from its members. The society is concerned with keeping up with and sharing the latest findings in all areas of criminology.

Federal Law Enforcement Society
PO Box 326
Lewisberry, PA 17339
(717) 938-2300
services@fleoa.org
http://www.fleoa.org

The Federal Law Enforcement Society represents more than 20,000 agents from 50 different federal law enforcement agencies. Founded in 1977, it is a non-partisan, professional organization that provides legal assistance and representation for its members. It also works to promote legislation that benefits federal law enforcement agents.

CRIMINOLOGIST

American Society of Criminology
1314 Kinnear Road
Columbus, OH 43212-1156

CRYONICS RESEARCHER

American Cryonics Society
PO Box 1509
Cupertino, CA 95015

(650)254-2001
cryonics@americancryonics.org
http://americancryonics.org

The American Cryonics Society offers cryonic suspension services and information.

Alcor Life Extension Foundation
7895 East Acoma Drive Suite 110
Scottsdale, AZ 85260
(480) 905-1906

The Alcor Life Extension Foundation is the world leader in cryonics, cryonics research, and cryonics technology.

Cryonics Institute
24355 Sorrentino Court
Clinton Township, MI 48035
(586) 791-5961
http://www.cryonics.org

The Cryonics Institute offers cryonic suspension services and information.

CRYPTOGRAPHER

American Mathematical Society
201 Charles Street
Providence, RI 02940
http://www.ams.org

Founded in 1888 to further mathematical research and scholarship, the American Mathematical Society fulfills its mission through programs and services that promote mathematical research and its uses, strengthen mathematical education, and foster awareness and appreciation of mathematics and its connections to other disciplines and to everyday life.

International Association of Cryptological Research
http://www.iacr.org

A nonprofit scientific organization whose purpose is to further research in cryptology and related fields. The Web site has information on events, international contacts, and jobs in the field.

Journal of Cryptology
55 Broad Street, Suite 22
New York, NY 10004
http://www.springeronline.com/sgw/cda/
frontpage/0,11855,4-164-70-1009426-
0,00.html

This journal provides a forum for original results in all areas of modern information security. Both cryptography and cryptanalysis are covered, including information on theoretic and complexity theoretic perspectives as well as implementation, application, and standards issues. Other topics include public key and conventional algorithms and their implementations, cryptanalytic attacks, pseudo-random sequences, computational number theory, cryptographic protocols, untraceability, privacy, authentication, key management and quantum cryptography. In addition to full-length technical, survey, and historical articles, the journal publishes short notes.

Society for Industrial and Applied Mathematics
3600 University City Science Center
Philadelphia, PA 19104-2688
http://www.siam.org

SIAM exists to ensure the strongest interactions between mathematics and other scientific and technological communities through membership activities, publication of journals and books, and conferences.

DOCUMENT EXAMINER

American Association of Handwriting Analysts
http://aaha-handwriting.org
An organization founded in 1962 with more than 300 members, offering seminars, conferences, and workshops, a lending library, and accreditation exams.

Handwriting Analysis
http://www.hwa.org
The original Web handwriting site.

National Association of Document Examiners
3490 U.S. Route 1 North, Suite 3B
Princeton, NJ 08540
(609) 452-7030
forgerynet@aol.com
http://expertpages.com/org/nade.htm

The National Association of Document Examiners, founded in 1980, is comprised of handwriting experts who examine signatures and documents to determine authenticity or identify the originator.

DOLPHIN RESEARCHER

Dolphin Communication Project
55 Coogan Boulevard
Mystic, CT 06355

The Dolphin Communication Project studies how dolphins communicate and attempts to shed more light on the meaning of their interactions. With research ongoing since 1991, questions focus on signal exchange in Bahamas' Atlantic spotted dolphins and Indo-Pacific bottlenose dolphins at Mikura Island, Japan with comparisons between species and geographies. The project

offers workshops, seminars, symposia and more.

The Dolphin Institute
420 Ward Avenue, Suite 212
Honolulu, HI 96814
(800) 831-8305
correspondence@dolphin-institute.org
http://www.dolphin-institute.org

Founded in 1993, this Hawaii-based not-for-profit organization is dedicated to the study and preservation of dolphins and whales, and to the education of people whose attitudes and activities affect the survival of these animals. The Dolphin Institute is associated with and supports the world-renowned dolphin and whale research center, the Kewalo Basin Marine Mammal Laboratory in Honolulu.

Kewalo Basin Marine Mammal Laboratory
1129 Ala Moana Boulevard
Honolulu, HI 96814
(808) 591-2121
correspondence@dolphin-institute.org
http://www.dolphin-institute.org

A world-renowned dolphin and whale research center in Honolulu that for 30 years has studied the behavioral capacities of dolphins, including how dolphins perceive their world, their intellectual potential, and their social life. The lab is home to the world's most educated dolphins, who are involved in research into their abilities to comprehend language, vocal and behavioral imitation, "imaging" of objects through echolocation, interpretation of television displays and scenes, and evidence of self-awareness.

Woods Hole Oceanographic Institute
Co-op Building, MS #16
Woods Hole, MA 02543

(508) 548-1400

http://www.whoi.edu

A private, nonprofit research facility dedicated to the study of marine science and to the education of marine scientists. It is the largest independent oceanographic institution in the world.

ENTOMOLOGIST

The American Entomological Association
1900 Benjamin Franklin Parkway
Philadelphia, PA 19103
(215) 561-3978
AES@acnatsci.org
http://www.acnatsci.org

The American Entomological Society was founded in 1859, the oldest continuously operating entomological society in the United States. The society's headquarters are located within the Academy of Natural Sciences of Philadelphia. Anyone with an interest in entomology may join; membership benefits include access to the society's comprehensive library, educational programs, conferences, seminars, family days, and more. The society works to support entomological research, education, and outreach.

The Amateur Entomologists' Society
PO Box 8774
London, England SW7 5ZG
Info@theaes.org
http://www.amentsoc.org

The Amateur Entomologists' Society (AES) is open to anyone who is interested in insects and the study of entomology. The AES has a division called The Bug Club, which is geared toward children and teens. The Bug Club includes an online discussion group, lots of information about insects and entomology, interactive activities, a newsletter, and other benefits. The AES sponsors educational and networking opportunities geared toward adults.

FINGERPRINT ANALYST

The International Association of Crime Analysts
9218 Metcalf Avenue, #364
Overland Park, KS 66212
(800) 609-3419
iaca@iaca.net
http://www.iaca.net

The International Association of Crime Analysts (IACA) was founded in 1990 to provide education, advocacy, and networking opportunities for crime analysts around the world. The organization has about 1,000 members from 31 countries, but the great majority of members are from the United States. In addition to crime analysts, its membership includes police officers, educators, intelligence analysts, and students. The IACA holds an annual conference, publishes newsletters for members, and recently wrote and published its first book, Exploring Crime Analysis.

International High Technology Crime Investigation Association
1474 Freeman Drive
Amissville, VA 20106
(540) 937-5019
exec_secty@htcia.org
http://www.htcia.org

The International High Technology Crime Investigation Association (HTCIA) is a networking forum for its members, which include professionals involved with all areas of criminology.

The HTCIA holds an annual training conference and exposition, with regional training conferences held at various times throughout the year. Members may submit articles for publication in the association's newsletter, and job openings in the field of crime investigation are posted on its Web site.

FIRE SCIENTIST

Association for Fire Ecology
Department of Environmental Science
and Policy
University of California, Davis
Davis, CA 95616
http://www.fireecology.net

The Association for Fire Ecology (AFE) is an organization of professionals dedicated to improving the knowledge and use of fire in land management. AFE is accomplishing these goals through developing symposia, short courses, and several projects that make up the California Fire Effects Information Resource. The Association for Fire Ecology was started by a group of researchers in California involved with the California Association for Fire Ecology (CAFE). In recognition of the need for fire ecology information at the national level, the Association for Fire Ecology was created. CAFE has now become a chapter of the larger national Association for Fire Ecology and is continuing with their state-level projects. Currently there are two chapters: CAFE and the Student Association for Fire Ecology.

International Association of Wildland Fire

PO Box 261
Hot Springs, SD 57747-0261
(605) 890-2348
http://www.iawfonline.org

This nonprofit, professional association represents members of the global wildland fire community. The purpose of the association is to facilitate communication and provide leadership for the wildland fire community.

Student Association for Fire Ecology
http://web1.spatial.wwu.edu/~afe/Safe/
webB/index.htm

The Student Association for Fire Ecology (SAFE) was formed by a group of graduate students from a variety of academic disciplines with a strong interest in fire ecology and related issues, including dendrochronology, fire behavior, ecosystem restoration, tropical fire ecology, indigenous fire management, fire-watershed processes, fire-wildlife interactions, and grassland conservation. The primary objective of SAFE is to provide graduate students from diverse backgrounds with an open forum on fire ecology through which research can be shared, networks formed, and funding and information resources can be accessed.

FLIGHT NURSE

Air & Surface Transport Nurses Association
7995 East Prentice Avenue, Suite 100
Greenwood Village, CO 80111
(800) 897-6362
astna@gwami.com
http://www.astna.org

The Air & Surface Transport Nurses Association (ASTNA) was known until 1998 as the National Flight Nurses Association. The mission of the non-profit organization is to advance the profession of transport nursing and to train nurses to provide the best possible patient care. ASTNA publishes a quarterly member newsletter, the bi-monthly Air Medical Journal, *and offers educational opportunities for its members. With about 1,750 members, the association also holds an annual conference.*

Emergency Nurse Association
915 Lee Street
Des Plaines, IL 60016
(847) 460-2630
enainfo@ena.org
http://www.ena.org

The Emergency Nurse Association (ENA) strives to promote excellence in emergency nursing through leadership, research, education, and advocacy. The association, with more than 23,000 members in more than 20 countries around the world, has established certification standards for emergency nurses and provides educational and testing opportunities. The ENA holds an annual conference and publishes journals and newsletters for its members.

FORENSIC SCULPTOR

International Association for Identification
2535 Pilot Knob Road, Suite 117
Mendota Heights, MN 55120-1120
(651) 681-8566

An international association dedicated to the advancement of forensic disciplines through education.

GEMOLOGIST

Accredited Gemologists Association
1115 S. 900 East
Salt Lake City, UT 84105
info@accreditedgemologists.org
http://accreditedgemologists.org

The Accredited Gemologists Association (AGA) is an international, nonprofit organization of gemologists and jewelers, organized in 1974 as an opportunity for gemologists to network and share information and skills. It's committed to education in the area of gemology, research, identifying and evaluating gems, and developing and maintaining professional standards within the area of gemology. The AGA holds an annual conference, publishes an annual journal, and offers educational opportunities for members.

Gemological Institute of America
The Robert Mouawad Campus
5345 Armada Drive
Carlsbad, CA 92008
(800) 421-7250
http://www.gia.edu

The Gemological Institute of America (GIA) was founded in 1931 to foster public trust in gems and jewelry by promoting the highest standards and qualifications for gemologists and jewelers. The nonprofit agency promotes integrity, academics, science, and professionalism for those in the gem and jewelry businesses, and offers education, research, and laboratory services. The GIA certification program establishes a gemologist as a senior professional in the jewelry field.

GERIATRIC CARE MANAGER

National Academy of Certified Care Managers
PO Box 669
244 Upton Road
Colchester, CT 06415-0669
(800) 962-2260
naccm@snet.net
http://www.naccm.net

The National Academy of Certified Care Managers (NACCM) was founded with the purpose of advancing the quality of care management services by establishing guidelines and certification requirements for service providers. The NACCM certifies care managers and provides ongoing education and training. The NACCM holds an annual conference and offers other benefits for its members.

National Association of Professional Geriatric Care Managers, Inc.
1604 North Country Club Road
Tucson, AZ 85716
(520) 881-8008
info@caremanager.org
http://www.caremanager.org

The National Association of Professional Geriatric Care Managers is a nonprofit association that works to advance the profession of geriatric care management and to help its members work for better social, psychological, and health care for the elderly and their families. Founded in 1985, the association sponsors an annual conference, offers a national member directory, local chapters that hold their

own meetings and seminars, legislative updates, and other services.

HERPETOLOGIST

American Society of Ichthyologists and Herpetologists
Florida International University
Biological Sciences
11200 SW 8th Street
Miami, FL 33199
(305) 348-1235
asih@fiu.edu
http://www.asih.org/index.html

This society is dedicated to the scientific study of fishes, amphibians, and reptiles. The primary emphases of the society are to increase knowledge about these organisms, to disseminate that knowledge through publications, conferences, symposia, and other means, and to encourage and support young scientists who will make future advances in these fields. The programs of the society are part of a global effort to interpret, understand, and conserve the Earth's natural diversity and to contribute to the wise use of natural resources for the long-term benefit of humankind.

Herpetologists' League
Box 70726
East Tennessee State University
Johnson City, TN 37614-0726
http://www.inhs.uiuc.edu/cbd/HL/HL.html

The Herpetologists' League, established in 1936, is an international organization of people devoted to studying the biology of amphibians and reptiles. The history of the first 50 years of the Herpetologists' League can be found in Hobart Smith's 1986 paper in Herpetologica: "Chapman Grant, Herpetologica, and the Herpetologists' League." HL publishes two scholarly journals—the quarterly Herpetologica, which contains original research papers, essays and book reviews, and the annual supplement Herpetological Monographs, which contains longer research articles, syntheses, and special symposia.

Society for the Study of Amphibians and Reptiles
303 West 39th Street
Hayes, KS 67601
http://www.ssarherps.org

A nonprofit organization established to advance research, conservation, and education concerning amphibians and reptiles, was founded in 1958. It is the largest international herpetological society, and is recognized worldwide for having the most diverse program of publications, meetings, and other activities.

HISTORICAL INTERPRETER

American Historical Association
400 A Street, SE
Washington, DC 20003-3889
(202) 544-2422
info@historians.org
http://www.historians.org

Founded in 1884, the American Historical Association is the largest historical association in the United States. It advocates for historians, monitors professional standards, promotes historical research, provides educational resources to its members, and works to ensure academic freedom. In addition to more than 14,000 professionals in the

area of history, the American Historical Association's membership includes teachers, businesses, libraries, schools, colleges, universities, and other groups that share an interest in, and concern for, the preservation of historical artifacts and the accurate portrayal of historical events. The association provides many benefits and opportunities for members.

The Association for Living Historical Farms and Agricultural Museums, Inc.
8774 Route 45 NW
North Bloomfield, OH 44450
(440) 685-4410 (fax; there is no phone contact)
webmaster@alhfam.org
http://www.alhfam.org

The Association for Living Historical Farms and Agricultural Museums (ALHFAM) was formed in Maryland as a corporation in 1972 to establish a means of communication for those in the area of historical interpretation, and to encourage research into and publication of historical matters. The association's Web site provides a variety of links to informative sites. The association sponsors a national conference, regional events, publications, and an online newsletter.

HOSPITAL CHAPLAIN

The Association for Clinical Pastoral Education, Inc.
1549 Clairmont Road, Suite 103
Decatur, GA 30033-4611
(404) 320-1472
www.acpe@acpe.edu
http://www.acpe.edu

The Association for Clinical Pastoral Education, Inc. was founded in 1925 and offers a multicultural and multi-faith program called clinical pastoral education. It serves all religions. The educational programs do not take place exclusively in classrooms, but in the clinical settings where ministry is served, including hospitals, prisons, nursing homes, and hospices. It is preferred that students of clinical pastoral education will have finished at least one year of formal theological training, but it is not always necessary.

The Association of Professional Chaplains
1701 East Woodfield Road, Suite 760
Schaumburg, IL 60173
(847) 240-1014
info@professionalchaplains.org
http://www.professionalchaplains.org

The Association of Professional Chaplains has nearly 4,000 members representing more than 150 faith groups. The association serves chaplains in all types of settings, and advocates for the spiritual care of all people in hospitals, rehabilitation centers, prisons, nursing homes, hospices, the military, and other institutions. The Association of Professional Chaplains was founded by Rev. Russell L. Dicks in 1946 as the American Protestant Hospital Association. Dicks was the author in 1939 of a book called The Art of Ministering to the Sick.

HYPNOTHERAPIST

American Hypnosis Association
18607 Ventura Boulevard, Suite 310
Tarzana, CA 91356
(818) 758-2747
http://www.hypnosis.edu/aha

A national association of hypnotherapists and other professionals interested in hypnosis and related fields. The association helps members stay current with the latest developments in the field of hypnotherapy, behavior modification, counseling law, and promotional strategies for marketing private practice.

The Hypnotherapy Association
14 Crown Street
Chorley
Lancashire
PR7 1DX
Great Britain
(+44) [0]1257 262124
http://www.thehypnotherapyassociation.co.uk

The Hypnotherapy Association is a nonprofit organization representing hypnotherapists in active practice. The association provides a directory of hypnotherapists together with information about hypnotherapy and hypnosis.

LAUGHTER THERAPIST

The Humor Project, Inc.
480 Broadway, Suite 210
Saratoga Springs, NY 12866
(518) 587-8770
info@humorproject.com
http://www.humorproject.com

The Humor Project, Inc. was started in 1977 by Saratoga Springs resident Joel Goodman, a popular speaker and consultant for businesses, hospitals, schools, and other institutions. The Humor Project seeks to improve the lives of people worldwide by introducing them to the benefits and joys of laughter.

The World Laughter Tour, Inc.
1159 South Creekway Court
Gahanna, OH 43230
(614) 855-4733
info@worldlaughtertour.com
http://www.worldlaughtertour.com

The World Laughter Tour, Inc. was established in 1998 by Steve Wilson, a psychiatrist who became intrigued with the use of laughter in Eastern cultures for medical and emotional purposes. Wilson designed a curriculum to train laughter therapists, and opened a "laughter school." More than 1,500 people have completed the course and are certified by The World Laughter Tour as laughter therapists.

MASSAGE THERAPIST

The American Massage Therapy Association
500 Davis Street, Suite 900
Evanston, IL 60201-4695
(877) 905-2700
info@amtamassage.org
http://www.amtamassage.org

The association represents more than 53,000 massage therapists in 27 countries, trying to establish massage therapy as integral to the maintenance of good health and complementary to other therapeutic processes. The association also works to advance the profession through ethics and standards, certification, school accreditation, continuing education, professional publications, legislative efforts, and public education.

National Certification Board for Therapeutic Massage and Bodywork
8201 Greensboro Drive, Suite 300

McLean, VA 22102
(800) 296-0664
http://www.ncbtmb.com

An independent, private, nonprofit organization formed to set high standards of ethical and professional practice through a recognized, credible credentialing program. NCBTMB also promotes the worth of National Certification to the public and the profession, maintains the quality of the National Certification Program, and requires continuing education to keep practitioners current with advances in the field. NCBTMB certifies massage therapists and bodyworkers on behalf of the profession.

MEDICAL AESTHETICIAN

American Beauty Association
15825 North 71st Street
Scottsdale, AZ 85254
(800) 868-4265
http://www.abbies.org

Professional association for those in the skin care and beauty business.

Society of Dermatology SkinCare Specialists
484 Spring Avenue
Ridgewood, NJ 07450-4624
(201) 670-4100
sdssorg@aol.com
http://www.sdss.tv

A professional organization for skin care specialists.

MEDICAL ILLUSTRATOR

The Association of Medical Illustrators
245 1st Street, Suite 1800

Cambridge, MA 02142
(617) 395-8186
hq@ami.org
http://medical-illustrators.org/contact.
php

An international organization founded in 1945 whose members are primarily medical illustrators and artists. Members create medical art, and also serve in consultant, advisory, educational, and administrative capacities in all aspects of bioscientific communications and visual education.

Medical Artists' Association of Great Britain
http://www.maa.org.uk/welcome.htm

The Medical Artists' Association, whose members are primarily medical illustrators, ensures a high standard of training for British medical artists and strives to apply them to new and evolving technologies to maintain the high professional standards in medical art.

MENTAL HEALTH ADVOCATE

National Alliance on Mental Illness
Colonial Place Three
2107 Wilson Boulevard, Suite 300
Arlington, VA 22201-3042
(703) 524-7600
http://www.nami.org

NAMI is a nonprofit, grassroots, self-help, support, and advocacy organization of consumers, families, and friends of people with severe mental illnesses, such as schizophrenia, schizoaffective disorder, bipolar disorder, major depressive disorder, obsessive-compulsive disorder, panic and other severe anxiety disorders, autism and pervasive developmental disorders, attention deficit/hyperactivity

disorder, and other severe and persistent mental illnesses that affect the brain. Founded in 1979 as the National Alliance for the Mentally Ill, NAMI today works to achieve equitable services and treatment for more than 15 million Americans living with severe mental illnesses, and their families. Hundreds of thousands of volunteers participate in more than 1,000 local affiliates and 50 state organizations to provide education and support, combat stigma, support increased funding for research, and advocate for adequate health insurance, housing, rehabilitation, and jobs for people with mental illnesses and their families.

National Mental Health Association
2001 North Beauregard Street
12th Floor
Alexandria, VA 22311
(703) 684-7722
http://www.nmha.org

The National Mental Health Association (NMHA) was founded in 1909 by Clifford W. Beers, who had been subjected to a series of terrible abuses as a patient in psychiatric facilities. Beers founded the organization as a means of making people aware of the abuses within the mental health system. The goal of the NMHA is to educate the public about mental illness and provide advocacy services for mentally ill patients. The association has many affiliate chapters throughout the country, and provides hot lines, information, and other services.

MIDWIFE

The American College of Nurse-Midwives

8403 Colesville Road, Suite 1550
Silver Spring, MD 20910
(240) 485-1800
http://www.midwife.org

The American College of Nurse-Midwives was founded in 1955, and serves to teach, support, and empower certified nurse-midwives and certified midwives throughout the United States. The organization sponsors research, evaluates and accredits midwife training programs, encourages continuing education for its members, sets clinical practice standards, and establishes liaisons with state and federal agencies. It has state and regional chapters and publishes a newsletter and a journal.

Canadian Association of Midwives
#207-2051 McCallum Road
Abbotsford BC V2S 3N5
CANADA
(604) 859-0777
admin@canadianmidwives.org
http://www.canadianmidwives.org

MUSEUM DISPLAY DESIGNER

American Association of Museums
1575 Eye Street NW, Suite 400
Washington, DC 20005
(202) 289-1818
info@aam-us.org
http://www.aam-us.org

The American Association of Museums (AAM), founded in 1906, works with museums across the country to provide the best possible facilities for the public. More than 3,100 museums across the country are members of the AAM, including art museums, zoos, aquariums, historical sites, technology centers, history museums, science centers,

military and maritime museums, and others.

Grandfather Mountain
PO Box 129
2050 Blowing Rock Highway
Linville, NC 28646
(800) 468-7325
nature@grandfather.com
http://www.grandfather.com

Grandfather Mountain is a nature preserve and center located on the highest peak of the Blue Ridge Mountain range. Among the attractions of Grandfather Mountain is a nature museum, which is noted for its impressive displays of gems and other natural objects. The displays are the work of Rolland Hower, former chief of natural history exhibits for the Smithsonian Institution.

PALLIATIVE CARE PROFESSIONAL

Association for Death Education and Counseling
60 Revere Drive, Suite 500
Northbrook, IL 60062
(847) 509-0403
http://www.adec.org

One of the oldest interdisciplinary organizations in the field of dying, death, and bereavement. Members include mental and medical health personnel, educators, clergy, funeral directors, and volunteers. ADEC offers numerous educational opportunities through its annual conference, courses and workshops, its certification program, and via its newsletter The Forum.

Hospice and Palliative Nurses Association

One Penn Center West, Suite 229
Pittsburgh, PA 15276
(412) 787-9301
http://www.hpna.org/approved_
educators.asp

*The Hospice and Palliative Nurses
Association (HPNA) exchanges
information, experiences, and ideas;
promotes understanding of the specialties
of hospice and palliative nursing; and
promotes hospice and palliative nursing
research. HPNA promotes the highest
professional standards of hospice and
palliative nursing; encourages nurses
to specialize in the practices of hospice
and palliative nursing; and promotes the
recognition of hospice and palliative care
as essential components throughout the
health care system.*

**National Hospice and Palliative Care
Organization**
1700 Diagonal Road, Suite 625
Alexandria, VA 22314
(703) 837-1500
http://nhpco.org

*National nonprofit organization that
works for social change for improved
care at the end of life.*

PARASITOLOGIST

The American Society of Parasitologists
NOSPAM-slg@unl.edu
http://asp.unl.edu

*The American Society of Parasitologists
was founded in 1924, and today is a
group of more than 1,500 scientists
working in academia, government, and
industry fields to advance the field of
parasitology. Its members are active in
research regarding parasites, in teaching
parasitology, and in applying parasitology*

*to various fields and areas. The American
Society of Parasitologists publishes a
bi-monthly journal that is aimed at
keeping members informed of recent
developments in the field of parasitology,
regional meetings and events, and
legislation which could affect funding or
otherwise have an effect on the field.*

**The American Association of Veterinary
Parasitologists**
Phoenix Scientific, Inc.
3915 S. 48th St. Terrace
St. Joseph, MO 64503-4711
(816) 364-3777, ext. 1375
amarchiondo@psiqv.com
http://www.aavp.org

*The American Association of Veterinary
Parasitologists (AAVP) was organized
in 1956. An educational and scientific
organization, it is affiliated with
the American Veterinary Medical
Association. Its 450 members work
to find ways to control, treat, prevent,
and diagnose parasites in both wild and
domestic animals, mindful that some of
these parasites can be spread to humans.
Membership includes veterinarians,
scientists, teachers, students, and others.
The AAVP holds an annual meeting every
July, at which time members and guests
present their latest research findings
regarding parasites in animals.*

PERFUSIONIST

**American Academy of Cardiovascular
Perfusion**
PO Box 3596
Allentown, PA 18106-0596
(610) 395-4853
http://users.aol.com/OfficeAACP/home.
html

The American Academy of Cardiovascular Perfusion was founded in 1979 to encourage investigation and study into cardiovascular perfusion.

American Society for Extra-Corporeal Technology

2209 Dickens Rd
PO Box 11086
Richmond, VA 23230-1086
(804) 565-6363
http://www.amsect.org

The mission of AmSECT is to foster improved patient care by providing for the continuing education and professional needs of the extracorporeal circulation technology community.

International Perfusion Association

Perfusion.com, Inc.
500 Keenan Avenue
Fort Myers, FL 33919-3120
http://www.perfusion.com/perfusion/ipa

The mission of the International Perfusion Association (IPA) is to provide the professional, educational, and communication resources necessary to foster the expansion of the perfusionist scope of practice and to improve the quality of patient care worldwide. The IPA serves as the governing body of Perfusion.com, and regulates all the educational, charitable, and organizational information and resources on the Perfusion.com Web site. The IPA is the largest professional organization representing cardiovascular perfusionists.

PHLEBOTOMIST

American Society for Clinical Pathology

2100 West Harrison Street

Chicago, IL 60612
(312) 738-1336
info@ascp.org
http://www.ascp.org

The American Society for Clinical Pathology (ASCP) was founded in 1922 to promote education concerning pathology and related fields. The not-for-profit organization's membership includes 11,000 pathologists and other physicians, and more than 129,000 laboratory professionals. The society sponsors more than 500 courses each year for medical laboratory personnel, and runs certification programs in a variety of areas, including phlebotomy. The ASCP has its own publishing arm, the ASCP Press, which is a full-scale medical publisher. The association also publishes two journals and a newsletter for members.

The American Society of Phlebotomy Technicians

PO Box 1831
Hickory, NC 28603
(828) 294-0078
office@aspt.org
http://www.aspt.org

The American Society of Phlebotomy Technicians (ASPT) was founded in 1983. Its primary goals are to test and certify phlebotomists, and to provide the necessary materials and opportunities for continuing education and study for phlebotomists. The organization also works to promote the professionalism of the phlebotomy field by encouraging all phlebotomists to work toward certification, even if it is not required for their jobs. The ASPT also publishes a newsletter for members and sponsors regional events.

PHYSICAL THERAPIST

American Physical Therapy Association
1111 North Fairfax Street
Alexandria, VA 22314-1488
(703) 684-2782
info@apta.org
http://www.apta.org

The American Physical Therapy Association (APTA) traces its roots back to 1921, when a physical therapist named Mary McMillan founded the American Women's Physical Therapeutic Association. Near the end of the 1930s the name had been changed to the American Physiotherapy Association and men were admitted. Today, the organization has more than 66,000 members. It works for advancements to improve research, education, and the practice of physical therapy. The APTA provides advocacy services for members, several publications, and educational and research opportunities.

Journal of Physical Therapy Education
1111 North Fairfax Street
Alexandria VA 22314
(800) 999-2782, x3237
http://www.aptaeducation.org/jopte/jopte.html

The Journal of Physical Therapy Education is peer reviewed and published three times each year by the Education Section of the American Physical Therapy Association.

SCIENTIFIC INVENTOR

National Congress of Inventor Organizations
PO Box 931881
Los Angeles, CA 90093-1881
(323) 878-6952
ncio@inventionconvention.com
http://www.inventionconvention.com/ncio

The NCIO was founded in the 1970s as a collaborative effort between government agencies and the private sector to come up with creative solutions to the oil crisis of that time. It became incorporated as a nonprofit organization in 1982. NCIO serves as a support for inventors and creative thinkers, offering an online inventors course and multiple sources of information concerning all aspects of inventing, including legal, patents, and other protections. It also offers a free online newsletter and inventors' updates.

SET MEDIC

National Association of Emergency Medical Technicians
PO Box 1400
Clinton, MS 39060
(800) 34-NAEMT
http://www.naemt.org

The oldest and largest national EMS trade association representing all EMTs and paramedics.

VENOM RESEARCHER

VenomousReptiles.org
http://www.venomousreptiles.org

A Web site dedicated to information about venomous reptiles, with articles, photos, information about antivenin, and much more.

VIROLOGIST

Centers for Disease Control and Prevention

1600 Clifton Road
Atlanta, GA 30333
(404) 639-3311
info@cdc.gov
http://www.cdc.gov

The Centers for Disease Control and Prevention (CDC) operates within the U.S. Department of Health and Human Services. Virologists work closely within the CDC to identify viruses and provide information to make the public aware of them. Originally founded in 1946 to help control malaria, the CDC works to promote public health and to prevent and control disease, accidents, workplace hazards, environmental health threats, and disabilities. The CDC's Web site contains a wealth of information about all types of viruses and other diseases, plus information on many other topics.

World Health Organization
Avenue Appia 20
1211 Geneva 27
Switzerland

(+ 41 22) 791 21 11
info@who.int
http://www.who.int

Established in 1948, the World Health Organization is the United Nations' health agency. Its mission is to attain the highest level of health for people around the world. Virologists work closely with the World Health Organization to monitor and treat viruses around the world. Of particular concern are HIV and the AIDS virus. The organization is governed by the World Health Assembly, which has 192 member states. The World Health Organization has regional offices for Africa, North and South America, Southeast Asia, Europe, the Eastern Mediterranean, and the Western Pacific.

APPENDIX B: ONLINE CAREER RESOURCES

This volume offers a look inside a wide range of unusual and unique careers that might appeal to someone interested in jobs in the health and science fields. And while it highlights general information, it's really only a glimpse into the job. The entries are intended to merely whet your appetite, and provide you with some career options you may never have known existed.

Before jumping into any career, you'll want to do more research to make sure that it's really something you want to pursue. You'll most likely want to learn as much as you can about the careers in which you are interested. That way, as you continue to research and talk to people in those particular fields, you can ask informed and intelligent questions that will help you make your decisions. You might want to research the education options for learning the skills you'll need to be successful, along with scholarships, work-study programs, and other opportunities to help you finance that education. Or you might want answers to questions that weren't addressed in the information provided here. If you search long enough, you can find just about anything using the Internet, including additional information about the jobs featured in this book.

✻ **A word about Internet safety:** The Internet is also a wonderful resource for networking. Many job and career sites have forums where students can inter-act with other people interested in and working in that field. Some sites even offer online chats where people can communicate with each other in real time. They provide students and jobseekers opportunities to make connections and maybe even begin to lay the groundwork for future employment. As you use these forums and chats, remember that anyone could be on the other side of that computer screen, telling you exactly what you want to hear. It's easy to get wrapped up in the excitement of the moment when you're on a forum or a chat, interacting with people who share your career interests and aspirations. Be cautious about what kind of personal information you make available on the forums and in the chats; never give out your full name, address, or phone number. Never agree to meet with someone you've met online.

SEARCH ENGINES

When looking for information, there are lots of search engines that will help you to find out more about these jobs, along with others that might interest you. While you might already have a favorite search engine, why not take some time to check out some of the others that are out there? Some have features that might help you find information not located with the others. Several engines will offer suggestions for ways to narrow your results, or related phrases you might want to search along with your search results. This is handy if you're having trouble locating exactly what you want.

Another good thing to do is to learn how to use the advanced search features of your favorite search engines. Knowing that might help you to zero in on exactly the information for which you are searching without wasting time looking through pages of irrelevant hits.

As you use the Internet to search information on the perfect career, keep in mind that, like anything else you find on the Internet, you need to consider the source from which the information comes.

Some of the most popular Internet search engines are:

AllSearchEngines.com
www.allsearchengines.com
This search engine index has links to the major search engines along with search engines grouped by topic. The site includes a page with more than 75 career and job search engines at http://www. allsearchengines.com/careerjobs.html.

AlltheWeb
http://www.alltheweb.com

AltaVista
http://www.altavista.com

Ask.com
http://www.ask.com

Dogpile
http://www.dogpile.com

Excite
http://www.excite.com

Google
http://www.google.com

HotBot
http://www.hotbot.com

LookSmart
http://www.looksmart.com

Lycos
http://www.lycos.com

Mamma.com
http://www.mamma.com

MSN Network
http://www.msn.com

My Way
http://www.goto.com

Teoma
http://www.directhit.com

Vivisimo
http://www.vivisimo.com

Yahoo!
http://www.yahoo.com

HELPFUL WEB SITES

The Internet is a wealth of information on careers—everything from the mundane to the outrageous. There are thousands of sites devoted to helping you find the perfect job for you, taking into account your interests, skills, and talents. The sites listed here are some of the most helpful ones the authors discovered while researching the jobs in this volume. The sites are listed in alphabetical order. They are offered for your information, and are not endorsed by the authors.

Absolute Arts
http://www.absolutearts.com

Absolute arts is the largest marketplace for contemporary art, art news, research, and art gallery and artist portfolios. Artists can add their Web site to the directory, participate in art discussion forums, learn more about art history (with the biographies of more than 22,000 artists, and more than 200,000 images from museums). You can sign up for the free e-mail newsletter, International Arts News, *at the site.*

All Experts

http://www.allexperts.com

"The oldest & largest free Q&A service on the Internet," AllExperts.com has thousands of volunteer experts to answer your questions. You can also read replies to questions asked by other people. Each expert has an online profile to help you pick someone who might be best suited to answer your question. Very easy to use, it's a great resource for finding experts who can help to answer your questions.

America's Career InfoNet

http://www.acinet.org

A wealth of information! You can get a feel for the general job market; check out wages and trends in a particular state for different jobs; learn more about the knowledge, skills, abilities, and tasks for specific careers; and learn about required certifications and how to get them. You can search more than 5,000 scholarship and other financial opportunities to help you further your education. A huge career resources library has links to nearly 6,500 online resources. For fun, you can take a break and watch one of nearly 450 videos featuring real people at work—everything from custom tailors to engravers, glassblowers to silversmiths.

Backdoor Jobs: Short-Term Job Adventures, Summer Jobs, Volunteer Vacations, Work Abroad and More

http://www.backdoorjobs.com

This is the Web site of the popular book by the same name, now in its third edition. While not as extensive as the book, the site still offers a wealth of information for people looking for short-term opportunities: internships, seasonal jobs, volunteer vacations, and work abroad situations. Job opportunities are classified into several categories: Adventure Jobs, Camps, Ranches & Resort Jobs, Ski Resort Jobs, Jobs in the Great Outdoors, Nature Lover Jobs, Sustainable Living and Farming Work, Artistic & Learning Adventures, Heart Work, and Opportunities Abroad.

Boston Works—Job Explainer

http://bostonworks.boston.com/globe/
job_explainer/archive.html

For nearly 18 months, the Boston Globe *ran a weekly series profiling a wide range of careers. Some of the jobs were more traditional, but with a twist, such as the veterinarian who makes house calls. Others were very unique and unusual, such as the profile of a leader of a society of monks. The profiles discuss an "average" day, challenges of the job, required training, salary, and more. Each profile gives an up-close, personal look at that particular career. In addition, the Boston Works Web site (http://bostonworks.boston.com) has a lot of good, general employment-related information.*

Career Guide to Industries

http://www.bls.gov/oco/cg/cgindex.htm

For someone interested in working in a specific industry, but who may be undecided about exactly what career to pursue, this site is the place to start. Produced by the U.S. Department of Labor, this site discusses working conditions, employment, occupations (in the industry), training and advancement, earnings, outlook, and sources of additional information.

Career Planning at About.com
http://careerplanning.about.com

Like most of the other About.com topics, the career planning area is a wealth of information, and links to other information on the Web. Among the excellent essentials are career planning A-to-Z, a career planning glossary, information on career choices, and a free career planning class. There are many great articles and other excellent resources.

Career Prospects in Virginia
http://www3.ccps.virginia.edu/career_prospects/default-search.html

Career Prospects is a database of entries with information about more than 400 careers. Developed by the Virginia Career Resource Network, the online career information resource of the Virginia Department of Education, Office of Career and Technical Education Services, was intended as a source of information about jobs "important to Virginia." It's actually a great source of information for anyone. While some of the information (such as wages, outlook, and some of the requirements) may apply only to Virginia, other information for each job, such as what it's like, getting ahead, skills, and links, will be of help to anyone interested in that career.

Career Voyages
http://www.careervoyages.gov

Billed as "the ultimate road trip to career success," this site is sponsored by the U.S. Department of Labor and the U.S. Department of Education. This site features sections for students, parents, career changers, and career advisors. The FAQ offers great information about getting started, the high-growth industries, how to find your perfect job, how to make sure you're qualified for the job you want, tips for paying for the training and education you need, and more. Also interesting are the hot careers *and the* emerging fields *sections.*

Dream Jobs
http://www.salary.com/careers/layouthtmls/crel_display_Cat10.html

The staff at Salary.com takes a look at some wild, wacky, outrageous, and totally cool ways to earn a living. The jobs they highlight include pro skateboarder, computer game guru, nose, diplomat, and much more. The profiles don't offer links or resources for more information, but they are informative and fun to read.

Find It! in DOL
http://www.dol.gov/dol/findit.htm

A handy source for finding information at the extensive U.S. Department of Labor Web site. You can "Find It!" by broad topic category, or by audience, which includes a section for students.

Fine Living: *Radical Sabbatical*
http://www.fineliving.com/fine/episode_archive/0,1663,FINE_1413_14,00.html#Series873

The show Radical Sabbatical *on the Fine Living network looks at people willing to take a chance and follow their dreams and passions. The show focuses on individuals between the ages of 20 and 65 who have made the decision to leave successful, lucrative careers to start over, usually in an unconventional career. You can read all about these people and their journeys on the show's Web site.*

Free Salary Survey Reports and Cost of Living Reports

http://www.salaryexpert.com

Based on information from a number of sources, Salary Expert will tell you what kind of salary you can expect to make for a certain job in a certain geographic location. Salary Expert has information on hundreds of jobs; everything from your more traditional white- and blue-collar jobs, to some unique and out of the ordinary professions like acupressurist, blacksmith, denture waxer, taxidermist, and many others. With sections covering schools, crime, community comparison, and community explorer, the moving center is a useful area for people who need to relocate for training or employment.

Fun Jobs

http://www.funjobs.com

Fun Jobs has job listings for adventure, outdoor, and fun jobs at ranches, camps, and ski resorts. The job postings have a lot of information about the position, requirements, benefits, and responsibilities so that you know what you are getting into ahead of time. And, you can apply online for most of the positions. The Fun Companies *link will*

let you look up companies in an A-to-Z listing, or you can search for companies in a specific area or by keyword. The company listings offer you more detailed information about the location, types of jobs available, employment qualifications, and more.

Girls Can Do

http://www.girlscando.com

"Helping Girls Discover Their Life's Passions," Girls Can Do has opportunities, resources, and a lot of other cool stuff for girls ages 8 to 18. Girls can explore sections on Outdoor Adventure, Sports, My Body, The Arts, Sci-Tech, Change the World, *and* Learn, Earn, and Intern. *In addition to reading about women in all sorts of careers, girls can explore a wide range of opportunities and information that will help them grow into strong, intelligent, capable women.*

Great Web Sites for Kids

http://www.ala.org/gwstemplate.cfm?section=greatwebsites&template=/cfapps/gws/default.cfm

Great Web Sites for Kids is a collection of more than 700 sites organized into a variety of categories, including animals, sciences, the arts, reference, social sciences, and more. All of the sites included here have been approved by a committee made up of professional librarians and educators. You can even submit your favorite great site for possible inclusion.

Hot Jobs: Career Tools Home

http://www.hotjobs.com/htdocs/tools/index-us.html

While the jobs listed at Hot Jobs are more on the traditional side, the Career Tools *area has a lot of great resources for anyone looking for a job. You'll find information about how to write a resume and a cover letter, how to put together a career portfolio, interviewing tips, links to career assessments, and much more.*

Job Descriptions & Job Details
http://www.job-descriptions.org

Search for descriptions and details for more than 13,000 jobs at this site. You can search for jobs by category or by industry. You'd probably be hard pressed to find a job that isn't listed here, and you'll probably find lots of jobs you never imagined existed. The descriptions and details are short, but it's interesting and fun, and might lead you to the career of your dreams.

Job Hunter's Bible
http://www.jobhuntersbible.com

This site is the official online supplement to the book What Color Is Your Parachute? A Practical Manual for Job-Hunters and Career-Changers, *and is a great source of information with lots of informative, helpful articles and links to many more resources.*

Job Profiles
http://www.jobprofiles.org

A collection of profiles where experienced workers share about rewards and stressful parts of their jobs; basic skills the jobs demand; challenges of the future; and advice on entering the field. The careers include everything from baseball ticket manager to pastry chef and much, much more. The hundreds of profiles are arranged by broad category. While most of the profiles are easy to read, you can check out the How to

Browse JobProfiles.org section (http://www.jobprofiles.org/jphowto.htm) if you have any problems.

Major Job Web sites at Careers.org
http://www.careers.org/topic/01_jobs_10.html

This page at the careers.org Web site has links for more than 40 of the Web's major job-related Web sites. While you're there, check out the numerous links to additional information.

Monster Jobs
http://www.monster.com

Monster.com is one of the largest, and probably best known, job resource sites on the Web. It's really one-stop shopping for almost anything job-related that you can imagine. You can find a new job, network, update your resume, improve your skills, plan a job change or relocation, and so much more. Of special interest are the Monster: Cool Careers *(http://change.monster.com/archives/coolcareers) and the* Monster: Job Profiles *(http://jobprofiles.monster.com) sections where you can read about some really neat careers. The short profiles also include links to additional information. The* Monster: Career Advice *section (http://content.monster.com/) has resume and interviewing advice, message boards where you can network, relocation tools and advice, and more.*

Occupational Outlook Handbook
http://www.bls.gov/oco

Published by the U.S. Department of Labor's Bureau of Labor Statistics, the Occupational Outlook Handbook *(sometimes referred to as the* OOH) *is the premiere source of career information. The book is updated every two years, so you can be assured that the*

information you are using to help make your decisions is current. The online version is very easy to use; you can search for a specific occupation, browse through a group of related occupations, or look through an alphabetical listing of all the jobs included in the volume. Each of the entries will highlight the general nature of the job, working conditions, training and other qualifications, job outlook, average earning, related occupations, and sources of additional information. Each entry covers several pages and is a terrific source to get some great information about a huge variety of jobs.

The Riley Guide: Employment Opportunities and Job Resources on the Internet
http://www.rileyguide.com

The Riley Guide is an amazing collection of job and career resources. Unless you are looking for something specific, one of the best ways to maneuver around the site is with the A-to-Z Index. You can find everything from links to careers in enology to information about researching companies and employers. The Riley Guide is a great place to find just about anything you might be looking for, and probably lots of things you aren't looking for. But, be forewarned, it's easy to get lost in the A-to-Z Index, reading about all sorts of interesting things.

USA TODAY Career Focus
http://www.usatoday.com/careers/dream/dreamarc.htm

Several years ago, USA TODAY ran a series featuring people working in their dream jobs. In the profiles, people discuss how they got their dream job, what they enjoy the most about it, they talk about an average day, their

education backgrounds, sacrifices they had to make for their jobs, and more. They also share words of advice for anyone hoping to follow in their footsteps. Most of the articles also feature links where you can find more information. The USATODAY.Com Job Center(http://www.usatoday.com/money/jobcenter/front.htm) also has links to lots of resources and additional information.

CAREER TESTS AND INVENTORIES

If you have no idea what career is right for you, there are many resources available online that will help assess your interests and maybe steer you in the right direction. While some of the assessments charge a fee, there are many out there that are free. You can locate more tests and inventories by searching for the keywords *career tests, career inventories,* or *personality inventories.* Some of the most popular assessments available online are:

Campbell Interest and Skill Survey (CISS)
http://www.usnews.com/usnews/edu/careers/ccciss.htm

Career Explorer
http://careerexplorer.net/aptitude.asp

Career Focus 2000 Interest Inventory
http://www.iccweb.com/careerfocus

The Career Interests Game
http://career.missouri.edu/students/explore/thecareerinterestsgame.php

The Career Key
http://www.careerkey.org

CAREERLINK Inventory
http://www.mpc.edu/cl/cl.htm

Career Maze
http://www.careermaze.com/home.
asp?licensee=CareerMaze

Career Tests at CareerPlanner.com
http://www.careerplanner.com

FOCUS
http://www.focuscareer.com

Keirsey Temperament Test
http://www.keirsey.com

Motivational Appraisal of Personal
Potential (MAPP)
http://www.assessment.com

Myers-Briggs Personality Type
http://www.personalitypathways.com/
type_inventory.html

Princeton Review Career Quiz
http://www.princetonreview.com/cte/
quiz/default.asp

Skills Profiler
http://www.acinet.org/acinet/skills_home.
asp

READ MORE ABOUT IT

The following sources and books may help you learn more about health and science careers.

GENERAL CAREERS

Brown, Sheldon S. *Opportunities in Biotechnology Careers*. New York: McGraw Hill, 2000.

Culbreath, Alice N. and Saundra K. Neal. *Testing the Waters: A Teen's Guide to Career Exploration*. New York: JRC Consulting, 1999.

Dawicki, Ed. *Adventures Unlimited: The Guide for Short-Term Jobs in Exotic Places*. Lincoln, Neb.: iUniverse, 2003.

Donaldson, Robert, Kathleen Lundgren, and Howard Spiro (eds). *The Yale Guide to Careers in Medicine and the Health Professions: Pathways to Medicine in the 21st Century*. New Haven: Yale University Press, 2003.

Farr, Michael, LaVerne L. Ludden, and Laurence Shatkin. *200 Best Jobs for College Graduates*. Indianapolis, Ind.: Jist Publishing, 2003.

Fasulo, Mike, and Jane Kinney. *Careers for Environmental Types & Others Who Respect the Earth*. New York: McGraw-Hill, 2001.

Field, Shelly. *Career Opportunities in Health Care* 2nd ed. New York: Facts on File, 2002.

Flowers, Lawrence O. *Science Careers: Personal Accounts from the Experts*. Lanham, Md.: Scarecrow Press, 2003.

Fogg, Neeta, Paul Harrington, and Thomas Harrington. *College Majors Handbook with Real Career Paths and Payoffs: The Actual Jobs, Earnings, and Trends for Graduates of 60 College Majors*. Indianapolis, Ind.: Jist Publishing, 2004.

Jakubiak, Joyce, ed. *Specialty Occupational Outlook: Trade and Technical*. Detroit: Gale Research, Inc., 1996.

Krannich, Ronald L., and Caryl Rae Krannich. *The Best Jobs for the 1990s and into the 21st Century*. Manassas Park, Va.: Impact Publications, 1995.

Kreeger, Karen Young. *Guide to Nontraditional Careers in Science*. New York: Taylor & Francis Group, 1998.

Robbins-Roth, Cynthia. *Alternative Careers in Science: Leaving the Ivory Tower*. Burlington, Ma.: Academic Press, 1998.

Wischnitzer, Saul, and Edith Wischnitzer. *Top 100 Health Care Careers: Your Complete Guidebook To Training And Jobs In Allied Health, Nursing, Medicine, And More*. 2nd ed. Indianapolis, Ind.: Jist Publishing, 2005.

ACUPUNCTURIST

Kidson, Ruth. *Acupuncture for Everyone: What It Is, Why It Works, and How It Can Help You*. Rochester, Vt.: Healing Arts Press, 2001.

Sollars, David W. *Complete Idiot's Guide to Acupuncture and Acupressure*. New York: Alpha, 2000.

AROMATHERAPIST

Catty, Suzanne. *Hydrasols: The Next Aromatherapy*. Rochester, Vt.: Healing Arts Press, 2001.

Lawless, Julia. *The Illustrated Encyclopedia of Essential Oils: The Complete*

Guide to the Use of Oils in Aromatherapy and Herbalism. London: Element Books, 1995.

Schnaubelt, Kurt. *Advanced Aromatherapy: The Science of Essential Oil Therapy*. Rochester, Vt.: Healing Arts Press, 1998.

Worwood, Valerie Ann. *The Complete Book of Essential Oils and Aromatherapy*. Novato, Calif.: New World Library, 1991.

ART THERAPIST

Moon, Catherine Hyland. *Studio Art Therapy: Cultivating the Artist Identity in the Art Therapist*. Philadelphia, Pa.: Jessica Kingsley Publishers, 2001.

Riley, Shirley. *Contemporary Art Therapy With Adolescents*. Philadelphia, Pa.: Jessica Kingsley Publishers, 1999.

Malchiodi, Cathy. *The Art Therapy Sourcebook*. New York: McGraw-Hill, 1998.

ASTRONAUT

Parks, Peggy. *Astronaut (Exploring Careers)*. Farmington Hills, Mich.: KidHaven Press, 2005.

Poskanzer, Susan Cornell. *What's It Like to Be an Astronaut (Young Careers)*. Berkeley, Calif.: Troll Communications, 1990.

ASTRONOMER

Dickinson, Terence. *Nightwatch: A Practical Guide to Viewing the Universe*. Richmond Hill, Ontario: Firefly Books, 1998.

Dickinson, Terence, and Alan Dyer. *The Backyard Astronomer's Guide*. Richmond Hill, Ontario: Firefly Books, 2002

CRIME SCENE EXAMINER

Walker, Pam, and Elaine Wood. *Crime Scene Investigations: Real-Life Science Labs for Grades 6-12*. Hoboken, N.J.: Jossey-Bass, 2002.

Wirths, Claudine. *Choosing a Career in Law Enforcement*. New York: Rosen Publishing Group, 1996.

CRIMINOLOGIST

Morgan, Marilyn. *Careers in Criminology*. New York: McGraw Hill, 2000.

Stinchcomb, James. *Opportunities in Law Enforcement and Criminal Justice Careers* (revised edition). New York: McGraw-Hill, 2002.

CRYONICS RESEARCHER

Kurzweil, Ray. *Fantastic Voyage: Live Long Enough to Live Forever*. Emmaus, Pa.: Rodale Books, 2004.

Perry, Michael R. *Forever For All: Moral Philosophy, Cryonics, and the Scientific Prospects for Immortality*. New South Wales, Australia: Universal Publishers, 2000.

CRYPTOGRAPHER

Haufler, Hervie. *Codebreakers' Victory: How the Allied Cryptogaphers Won World War II*. New York: New American Library, 2003.

Schneier, Bruce. *Applied Cryptography: Protocols, Algorithms, and Source Code in C.* New York: Wiley, 1995.

DOCUMENT EXAMINER
Santoy, Claude. *The ABC's of Handwriting Analysis: A Guide to Techniques and Interpretations.* New York: Marlowe & Company, 2001.

Branston, Barry. *Graphology Explained: A Workbook.* Boston: Weiser Books, 1991.

DOLPHIN RESEARCHER
Dudzinski, Kathleen. *Meeting Dolphins: My Adventures in the Sea.* Washington, D.C.: National Geographic Books, 2000.

Pryor, Karen, and Konrad Lorenz. *Lads Before the Wind: Diary of a Dolphin Trainer.* Waltham, Mass.: Sunshine Books, Inc., 2000.

Smolker, Rachel. *To Touch a Wild Dolphin: A Journey of Discovery with the Sea's Most Intelligent Creatures.* Nelson, New Zealand: Anchor, 2002.

ENTOMOLOGIST
Gullan, P.J., and P.S. Cranston. *The Insects: An Outline of Entomology.* Malden, Mass.: Blackwell Science, 2000.

White, Richard E. *A Field Guide to Insects.* Boston: Houghton Mifflin, 1998.

FINGERPRINT ANALYST
Cowger, James F. *Friction Ridge Skin: Comparison and Identification of Fingerprints.* Boca Raton, Fla.: CRC-Press, 1992.

International Association of Crime Analysts. *Exploring Crime Analysis: Reading on Essential Skills.* North Charleston, S.C.: BookSurge Publishing, 2005.

Jones, Gary W. *Introduction to Fingerprint Comparison.* Wildomar, Calif.: Staggs Publishing, 2000.

FIRE SCIENTIST
Agee, James K. *Fire Ecology of Pacific Northwest Forests.* Washington, D.C.: Island Press, 1996.

DeBano, Leonard F., Daniel G. Neary, and Peter F. Ffolliott. *Fire Effects on Ecosystems.* New York: Wiley, 1998.

Whelan, Robert J., H.J.B. Birks, and J.A. Wiens (eds). *The Ecology of Fire: Cambridge Studies in Ecology.* New York: Cambridge University Press, 1995.

FLIGHT NURSE
Hudson, Janice. *Trauma Junkie: Memoirs of an Emergency Flight Nurse.* Richmond Hill, Ontario: Firefly Books, Ltd., 2001.

Jensen, Pat. *Shock Trauma.* Winsted, Conn.: Willow River Books, 1997.

FORENSIC SCULPTOR
Camenson, Blythe. *Opportunities in Forensic Science Careers.* New York: McGraw-Hill, 2001.

Evans, Colin. *The Casebook of Forensic Detection: How Science Solved 100 of the World's Most Baffling Crimes.* New York: Wiley, 1998.

Jackson, Donna M. *The Bone Detectives: How Forensic Anthropologists Solve Crimes and Uncover Mysteries of the Dead*. New York: Little, Brown, 1996.

GEMOLOGIST

Hall, Cally, and Harry Taylor. *Smithsonian Handbooks: Gemstones*. Baldwin Park, Calif.: Gem Guides Book Company, 2002.

Lyman, Kennie. *Simon & Schuster's Guide to Gems and Precious Stones*. West Albany, N.Y.: Fireside Press, 1986.

GERIATRIC CARE MANAGER

Dreher, Barbara. *Communication Skills for Working With Elders*. New York: Springer Publishing Co., 1987.

Salamon, Michael J. *A Basic Guide to Working With Elders*. New York: Springer Publishing Co., 1986.

HERPETOLOGIST

Halliday, Tim, and Kraig Adler. *Encyclopedia of Reptiles and Amphibians*. New York: Facts on File, 1986.

Porter, Kenneth. *Herpetology*. Philadelphia: W.B. Saunders Company, 1972.

Stebbins, Robert C., and Nathan W. Cohen. *A Natural History of Amphibians*. Princeton, N.J.: Princeton University Press, 1995.

Zug, G.R. *Herpetology: An Introductory Biology of Amphibians and Reptiles*. New York: Academic Press, 1993.

HISTORICAL INTERPRETER

Hadden, Robert Lee. *Reliving the Civil War: A Reenactor's Handbook*. Mechanicsburg, Pa.: Stackpole Books, 1999.

Roth, Stacy F. *Past into Present: Effective Techniques for First-Person Historical Interpretation*. Chapel Hill, N.C.: University of North Carolina Press, 1998.

HOSPITAL CHAPLAIN

Mack, Ronald. *The Basics of Hospital Chaplaincy*. Longwood, Fla.: Xulon Press, 2003.

Tenbrook, Gretchen W. *Broken Bodies, Healing Hearts: Reflections of a Hospital Chaplain*. Binghamton, N.Y.: Haworth Press, 2000.

HYPNOTHERAPIST

Hammond, D. Corydon. *Handbook of Hypnotic Suggestions and Metaphors*. New York: W. W. Norton & Company, 1990.

Banyan, Calvin and Gerald F. Kein. *Hypnosis and Hypnotherapy: Basic to Advanced Techniques for the Professional*. St. Paul, Minn.: Abbot Publishing House, 2001.

LAUGHTER THERAPIST

Goodheart, Annette. *Laughter Therapy: How to Laugh About Everything in Your Life That Isn't Really Funny*. Oak Harbor, Ohio: Less Stress Press, 1994.

Klein, Allen. *The Healing Power of Humor*. Los Angeles: Tarcher Press, 1989.

MASSAGE THERAPIST

Holloway, Colleen. *Success Beyond Work: What Prosperous Massage Therapists Know--Minimum Work, Maximum Profits, and a Sellable Business*. Miami Beach, Fla.: Saramore Pub Co., 2003.

Riggs, Art. *Deep Tissue Massage: A Visual Guide to Techniques*. Berkeley, Calif.: North Atlantic Books, 2002.

MEDICAL AESTHETICIAN

Lees, Mark. *Skin Care: Beyond the Basics*. Albany, N.Y.: Milady, 2001.

Begoun, Paula. *Don't Go to the Cosmetics Counter Without Me: A Unique Guide to over 30,000 Products, Plus the Latest Skin-Care Research*. Seattle, Wash.: Beginning Press, 2000.

MEDICAL ILLUSTRATOR

Hodges, Elaine. *The Guild Handbook of Scientific Illustration*. New York: Wiley, 2003.

Wood, Phyllis. *Scientific Illustration: A Guide to Biological, Zoological, and Medical Rendering Techniques, Design, Printing, and Display*. New York: Wiley, 1994.

MENTAL HEALTH ADVOCATE

Hicks, James Whitney. *50 Signs of Mental Illness: A Guide to Understanding Mental Health*. New Haven, Conn.: Yale University Press, 2005.

Woolis, Rebecca. *When Someone You Love Has a Mental Illness*. New York: Tarcher, 1992.

MIDWIFE

Amstrong, Penny, and Sheryl Feldman. *A Midwife's Story*. New York: Arbor House Publishing Company, 1986.

van Olphen-Fehr, Juliana. *Diary of a Midwife: The Power of Positive Childbear-ing*. Westport, Conn.: Bergen & Garvey Trade, 1998.

MUSEUM DISPLAY DESIGNER

Camenson, B. *Opportunities in Museum Careers*. Lincolnwood, Ill.: VGM Career Horizons, 1996.

Yelavich, Susan, and Stephen Doyle. *Design for Life: Our Daily Lives, the Spaces We Shape, and the Ways We Communicate, As Seen Through the Collections of the Cooper Hewitt National Design Museum*. New York: Cooper Hewitt National Design Museum, 1997.

PALLIATIVE CARE TECHNICIAN

Beresford, Larry, and Elisabeth Kubler-Ross. *The Hospice Handbook: A Complete Guide*. New York: Little, Brown, 1993

Taylor, George Jesse, and Jerome E. Kurent (eds). *A Clinician's Guide to Palliative Care*. Malden, Mass.: Blackwell Publishers, 2002.

PARASITOLOGIST

Desowitz, Robert S. *The Malaria Capers: More Tales of Parasites and People, Research and Reality*. New York: W. W. Norton & Co., 1993.

Matthews, Bernard E. *An Introduction to Parasitology*. Cambridge, U.K.: Cambridge University Press, 1998.

PERFUSIONIST

Miles, Kenneth. *Perfusion CT: Applications in Oncology*. New York: Taylor & Francis Group, 2006.

Sorensen, Gregory A. *Cerebral Perfusion Imaging: Principles and Current Applications*. New York: Thieme Medical Publishers, 2001.

PHLEBOTOMIST
Garza, Diana, and Kathleen Becan-McBride. *Phlebotomy Handbook: Blood Collection Essentials*. 6th ed. Upper Saddle River, N.J.: Prentice Hall, 2002.
Fremgen, Bonnie F. and Wendy M. Blume. *Phlebotomy Basics: With Other Laboratory Techniques*. Upper Saddle River, N.J.: Prentice Hall, 2000.

PHYSICAL THERAPIST
Pagliarulo, Michael A. *Introduction to Physical Therapy*. St. Louis, Mo.: C.V. Mosby, 2001.
Vickery, Steve, and Marilyn Moffat. *The American Physical Therapy Association of Body Maintenance and Repair*. New York: Owl Books, 1999.

SCIENTIFIC INVENTOR
Krake, Don. *Turn Your Idea or Invention Into Millions*. New York: Allworth Press, 2001.
Louis, Ronald. *The Inventor's Bible: How to Market and License Your Brilliant Ideas*. Berkeley, Calif.: Ten Speed Press, 2001.
Pressman, David. *Nolo's Patents for Beginners*. 2nd. ed. New York: HarperCollins, 2001.

SET MEDIC
Honthaner, Eve Light. *The Complete Film Production Handbook (Book & CD-ROM)*. Burlington, Mass.: Focal Press, 2001.
Wilson, Mark. *The Medic's Guide to Work and Electives around the World*. London: Hodder Arnold, 2004.

VENOM RESEARCHER
Klaassen, Curtis D. *Casarett & Doull's Toxicology: The Basic Science of Poisons*. New York: McGraw-Hill Professional, 2001.
Meier, Jurg, and Julian White. *Handbook of Clinical Toxicology of Animal Venoms and Poisons*. Boca Raton, Fla.: CRC-Press, 1995.
Stocker, Kurt F. *Medical Use of Snake Venom Proteins*. Boca Raton, Fla.: CRC Press, 1990.
Tu, Anthony. *Handbook of Natural Toxins*. Boca Raton, Fla.: CRC Press, 1991.

VIROLOGIST
Primrose, A. *Introduction to Modern Virology*. Malden, Mass.: Blackwell Science, Inc., 1990.
Smith, Kenneth Manley. *Introduction to Virology*. New York: Wiley, 1980.

INDEX

A

ABFDE. *See* American Board of Forensic Document Examiners (ABFDE)
acupuncturist **1–3**, 123
Alcor Life Extension Foundation 23
All Criminal Justice Schools (Web site) 19
American Art Therapy Association 7
American Board of Forensic Document Examiners (ABFDE) 28
American Institute of Hypnosis 69
American Medical Technologists 101
American Pacific University 68
American Physical Therapy Association 104
American Society for Clinical Pathology 101
American Society for Phlebotomy Technicians 101
Amsterdam, University of 26
aromatherapist **4–6**, 123–124
Aromatherapy Registration Council 4, 6
art therapist **7–9**, 124–125

Art Therapy Credentials Board (ATCB) 7
Ashi Aromatics 5
associations, organizations, and Web sites xiii–xiv, 123–141
astronaut **10–12**, 125
astronomer **13–15**, 125
theorist 13
ATCB. *See* Art Therapy Credentials Board (ATCB)
Atlanta Braves 68
Atlantic Cetacean Research Center 32
Auburn University 47

B

Bell Labs Computing Sciences Research Center 26
Bingham, Jon-Paul x–xi
Board of Certification of Medical Illustrators 79
Boston University 59
Bush, George W. 30

C

California, University of at Berkeley 60
career tests and inventories 149–150
Charles Hayden Planetarium 62
Chicago, University of 26, 60
CIA 19, 26, 72

circulation technologist. *See* perfusionist
Clarkson University 117
College Notre-Dame-de-Foy, Canada 30
Colorado, University of Health Sciences Center 2
Commission on Accreditation in Physical Therapy Education 104
Commission on Massage Training Accreditation 74
Connecticut, University of 32
Cooke, Jim 62
Coolidge, Calvin 62
Copeia 60
Cornell University 60
crime scene examiner **16–18**, 125–126
criminologist **19–21**, 126
cryonics researcher **22–24**, 126–127
cryptanalysis 25, 27
cryptographer **25–27**, 127
cryptology 25
CSI: Crime Scene Investigation (TV show) 16, 20, 39

D

DCP. *See* Dolphin Communication Project (DCP)

Depp, Johnny 113
document examiner **28–30**, 128
  forensic document examiner 28
  handwriting analysts and experts 28–29
DOE Network 49
Dolphin Communication Project (DCP) 33
dolphin researcher **31–34**, 128–129
Dolphins (film) 33
Duke University 60

E
Ecological Restoration Institute (ERI) 42, 43
emergency medical technician (EMT) 112, 115
entomologist **35–37**, 129
ERI. *See* Ecological Restoration Institute (ERI)

F
Federal Bureau of Investigation (FBI) 18, 19, 38, 39, 72
Federal Emergency Management Agency 55
FFA. *See* Future Farmers of America (FFA)
fingerprint analyst **38–40**, 129–130
fire scientist **41–43**, 130
flight nurse **44–46**, 130–131
Flipper (TV show) 31
Florida Department of Law Enforcement 18
Florida, University of 60

Forensic Document Examination Course 29
forensic document examiner 28
forensic sculptor **47–49**, 131
Franklin, Benjamin 61–62
Future Farmers of America (FFA) 32

G
Galileo 62
Gates, Bill 110
Gatliff, Betty Pat 48–49
Gemological Institute of America (GMA) 51, 52
gemologist **51–53**, 131–132
general careers 151
General Motors 72
geriatric care manager **54–56**, 132
Glacier Tek, Inc. 109
GMA. *See* Gemological Institute of America (GMA)
Grandfather Mountain Nature Museum 90

H
handwriting analysts and experts 28–29
Harbor Press 69
Harvard University 60
Herpetologica 60
herpetologist **57–60**, 132–133
Hewlett-Packard 26
historical interpreter **61–63**, 133
Hope Diamond exhibit 90

hospital chaplain **64–66**, 133–134
Hubble Space Telescope Key Project team 14
Humor Project 73
hypnotherapist **67–70**, 134

I
IATSE, local 767 113
IBM 26, 72
integrated pest management (IPM) 35

J
Johnson Space Center 10, 11
Journal of Herpetology 60

K
Kamen, Dean 108, 110
Kansas, University of 60

L
Laboratory of Reptile Ethology 59
laughter therapist **71–73**, 134–135
Law and Order (TV show) 16
Lucent Technologies 26

M
Marine Mammal Protection Act 31
massage therapist **74–76**, 135
medical aesthetician **77–78**, 135
Medical College of Georgia 81

Medical College of Virginia 81
medical illustrator **79–82,** 135–136
mental health advocate 83–85, 136
Miami/Dade Metropolitan Police Institute 18
Michigan, University of 60
midwife **86–88,** 136–137
Mile-High Swinging Bridge 90
Minnesota, University of 36
MorningStar Birth Services 87
Mount Sinai Medical Center 93
museum display designer **89–91,** 137
Museum of Science (Boston) 62

N
NADE. *See* National Association of Document Examiners (NADE)
NASA 11, 14
  Space Grant Consortia 12
National Academy of Certified Geriatric Care Managers 54
National Association for Holistic Aromatherapy 4, 5
National Association of Document Examiners (NADE) 29

National Board for Certification of Hospice and Palliative Nurses (NBCHPN) 92
National Certification Board for Therapeutic Massage and Bodywork (NCBTMB) 74–75
National Certification Commission for Acupuncture and Oriental Medicine 1
National Geographic Television 59
National Guard 30
National Guild of Hypnosis 69
National Institutes of Health 23
National Optical Astronomy Observatory (NOAO) 14
National Science Foundation 32
NAU. *See* Northern Arizona University (NAU)
NBCHPN. *See* National Board for Certification of Hospice and Palliative Nurses (NBCHPN)
NCBTMB. *See* National Certification Board for Therapeutic Massage and Bodywork (NCBTMB)
New York Maritime College 11
NOAO. *See* National Optical Astronomy Observatory (NOAO)

Northern Arizona University (NAU) 42
nurse 112–113

O
Occupational Outlook Handbook xii, xiii
online career resources xiv, 143–150
  career tests and inventories 149–150
  helpful Web sites 144–149
  search engines 143–144
Original Cool Vest 109
Otterbein College 59

P
palliative care professional **92–94,** 137–138
Palm Bay Police Department 18
paramedic 112
parasitologist **95–97,** 138
Patch Adams (film) 71
Penn State Hershey Medical Center 81
Pennsylvania, University of 20
Pennsylvania School of Muscle Therapy 75
perfusionist **98–100,** 138–139
Perry Mason (TV show) 29
phlebotomist **101–103,** 139
physical therapist **104–107,** 140
Pirates of the Caribbean II (film) 113

Portland State University
81

R
Reading Hospital 65
Reed College 81
Registered Aromatherapist
(R.A.) credential 4, 6

S
Sagan, Carl, 13
scientific inventor **108–111**, 140
search engines 143–144
Secret Service 19
Segway Human
Transporter 108
set medic **112–115**, 140
Shellfish Diseases
Research Program 96
Skin Care Aesthetics of
Chestnut Hill 78
Smithsonian Institution
90
Snow, Clyde 48
Space Grant Consortia,
NASA 12

T
Tennessee, University of
49, 59
Texas, University of, at
Arlington 60
Texas, University of, at
Austin 60
Texas Tech 81
theorist 13
Tulane Regional Primate
Research Centers 121
Tulane University Health
Sciences Center 121

U
United Way 84
U.S. Air Force 44
U.S. Armed Forces 12
U.S. Bureau of Alcohol,
Tobacco, Firearms and
Explosives 18, 19
U.S. Bureau of Labor
Statistics xii
U.S. Department of the
Interior 19
U.S. Food and Drug
Administration 23, 118

U.S. Patent and
Trademark Office 109
U.S. Postal Service 19

V
Vanderbilt LifeFlight 45
venom researcher **116–119**, 140
virologist **120–122**, 141

W
W.B. Saunders 81
Wilson, Steve 72
Wisconsin, University of,
at Madison 36
Worcester Polytechnic
Institute 108
World Laughter Tour,
Inc., The 72, 73

Y
Yale University 42